9034306   SNAILHAM, R.   SANGAY
                 5.50   SURVIVED
                                     986·64

Río Putumayo

0   100

- - - - - - - - - Frontier
+ + + + + + + Guayaquil-Q
_____ Pan American
▲ Principal volcanoes

Sangay Survived

Richard Snailham

Sangay Survived

The story of the Ecuador volcano disaster

Hutchinson of London

Hutchinson & Co. (Publishers) Ltd
3 Fitzroy Square, London W1P 6JD

London Melbourne Sydney Auckland
Wellington Johannesburg and agencies
throughout the world

First published 1978

Set in Monotype Garamond

Printed in Great Britain by The Anchor Press Ltd
and bound by Wm Brendon & Son Ltd, both of
Tiptree, Essex

ISBN 0 09 133390 3

Contents

To the memory of
ADRIAN ASHBY-SMITH, 1952–1976,
and
RONALD MACE, 1947–1976

Illustrations

Looking back over the way we came to the mountain
Minard L. Hall's aerial photographs showing Sangay
   from the north, its northern flank, its three craters,
   and the explosion crater after the eruption
Gerardo and Adrian make ready for the climb
At first we hacked up cold mud-ash

Between pages 144 and 145
Nick tapping in marker flags for our return
After the disaster we lost our way down similar couloirs
With shattered right arms the author and Peter Chadwick
   await rescue
Gerardo greets the author and Peter at Riobamba
   (*Associated Press*)
John Blashford-Snell, who set up an information centre,
   appearing in 'This is Your Life' (*Thames Television*)
Nick Cooke and his George Medal

IN THE TEXT

Acknowledgements

Of the famous institutions which enabled the British Vulcan Expedition Reconnaissance to get under way, I should like first to thank the Royal Society for its grant to Dr Peter Francis, and the Royal Geographical Society and the Mount Everest Foundation, who gave money and other forms of encouragement to the enterprise.

The Royal Engineers Mountaineering and Exploration Society and the Open University were the first to promote the idea of our geological work in the Andes, and the Pacific Steam Navigation Company generously carried two of our members to Guayaquil free of charge. The Scientific Exploration Society approved and supported us and, together with the Junior Leaders Regiment, Royal Engineers, was of great help after the tragedy. The Ministry of Defence also rallied round during our last days in Quito. For what was done for us after our return the debt, especially of Jan Iwandziuk and myself, to the surgeons, doctors, nurses and other staff of the Royal Herbert Hospital (now the Queen Elizabeth Memorial Hospital), Woolwich, is considerable. A great number of other institutions, firms and individuals gave generously in the preparatory stages of the expedition. We thank them all.

In Ecuador we were especially grateful to Ingeniero Carlos Mosquera and all his staff at the *Dirección General de Geología y Minas* for their unfailing support, to the *Ministerio de Relaciones Exteriores*, who gave us permission to carry out our reconnaissance, to the Ecuadorean army (commander-in-chief, General de Brigada Luis G. Durán) – and in particular the Special Forces of the *Brigada 'Patria' No. 1*, who, together with the Ecuadorean air force (commander-in-chief, Brigadier General Luis A. Franco), were so vital to our rescue. We owe much to Dr Minard Hall of the *Escuela Politécnica Nacional*, to Haroun Tazieff and his team, to Drs Herbert Reyes and Guillermo Guerra and all the staffs of the Andrade Marín and Vozandes hospitals and the Pichincha Clinic, to the late Dr Brian Kennerley and his wife, Margaret, and Dr Jeff Aucott of the *Proyecto Geológico de Gran Bretaña*, to Allan Miller, and finally – but perhaps principally – to Group-Captain Peter Wills and his family, Miss Terry Newenham, and all the rest of the staff of the British Embassy in Quito.

Invidious though it may seem, it would be unfair not to single out certain individuals who played a valuable part in the whole affair: Lieutenant-Colonels John Blashford-Snell and David Hall; Captain Angus Murray of the Pacific Steam Navigation Company; John Hemming, Director and Secretary of the Royal Geographical Society; Kenneth Monk of Gestetner Duplicators Ltd; Colonel Gordon Small, lately of the Royal Herbert Hospital, Woolwich; and Miss E. Zemla.

As far as the production of this book is concerned I have some personal thanks to add. Because I was not able to make any notes after 12 August 1976, my dependence on other people in gathering material has been all the greater.

I owe much to Nick Cooke and Jeff Aucott for their tape-recorded reminiscences and to Peter Chadwick, Nick Cooke and Sarah Iwandziuk for their written memories, many of which must have been painful to them.

Brian and Yvonne Ashby-Smith, Geneviève and Patrick Griffith, Jeannine Mace, Allan Miller, Captain Angus Murray, Rosemary Sharp of the *Daily Telegraph*, Dr Freddie Walker and Caroline Whitefoord all gave me useful information.

Dr Peter Francis, Lieutenant-Colonel David Hall and Group-Captain Peter Wills wrote reports which have been helpful, and Dr Minard Hall generously let me use his aerial photographs of Sangay.

My scientific ignorance was revealed when a small boy

at a lecture asked me whether Sangay was acidic or basic (he implied that all volcanoes were chemically one or the other so I couldn't get away with 'well, of course, we were only there for about a week', or 'it's very cloudy in that part of the Andes, you know'). So I am further indebted to Peter Francis for helping me with the scientific aspects of the work and for steering me away from the worst volcanological gaffes.

Since my return from Ecuador the Royal Military Academy, Sandhurst, has, as ever, been indulgent of my pre-occupation with this story, and I thank Donald Moss, the Director of Studies, and others in authority there. I had much help from Jim Quibell and others of the library staff, and also from the Royal Geographical Society library.

The extracts from 'the lesson of the moth' from *archy and mehitabel* by Don Marquis, copyright 1927 by Doubleday & Company Inc, are reproduced by permission of Doubleday & Company Inc, New York, and of Faber and Faber Ltd, London.

Author's Preface

On 12 August 1976, six Englishmen set off from their base camp at the foot of a snow-covered mountain in south-eastern Ecuador. They were carrying out the reconnaissance for a scientific expedition, the British Vulcan Expedition, which intended the following year to collect gases and rock samples from three volcanoes in the eastern cordillera of the Andes.

The first objective of the six was to climb Sangay, at 17496 feet (about 5230 metres) the highest consistently active volcano in the world. A week later two of them were dead and the four others were in hospitals in Quito, the country's capital. Most victims of volcanic eruptions are the innocent inhabitants of the immediate area of the mountain. Few are killed while consciously climbing to the volcano's summit. This is the story of such a tragedy, accidental and yet in a sense invited.

To be rained on by rocks in an eruption is an experience not, thankfully, given to many people. This book, in part, tries to show what it is like. But it is only a small part of the account because, like many a hot moment in battle, the trauma is fleeting. The rest of it tells how the six men came to be there at all, and what befell them in the dreadful times they endured shortly after mid-day on 12 August.

At the very same moment syndicates of rich men were setting out over the Scottish moors, their Purdeys tucked under their arms, to pepper the unsuspecting grouse. In the inconsequential way that these things have, this trivial irony came to my mind as we turned to face up to the horror of our situation on Sangay. For some enthusiasts in Britain it was the opening of a new season; for a little party of Britons in Ecuador it was very much the end of one.

Another parallel which occurred to us at an early stage in our sojourn on the flanks of the volcano was to the Uruguayan Rugby team whose plane crashed in the Chilean Andes in 1972. There were we, too, marooned in the high cordillera. Scrupulously there was no talk about this – the notion of cannibalism was too grisly, I suppose.

Nevertheless, some aspects of our fate were gruesome enough. Where they were I have had to take into account the sensibilities of the families and friends of the dead, and so the story is in places muted. In other respects – with the tiny exception of the expression of some views in dialogue form – nothing in this book departs from the truth as I vividly recall it or was told of it.

The Team

Lieutenant Adrian J. ASHBY-SMITH, RAOC, 23:
Expedition Quartermaster.

Adrian was born at Thetford, Norfolk. His parents soon moved
to Surrey and he was educated at Winton House Preparatory
School, and The Trinity School of John Whitgift, Croydon,
where he became a pillar of the CCF, particularly active in
encouraging shooting. He entered the RMA, Sandhurst, in 1971
and was commissioned into the Royal Army Ordnance Corps in
1973. Whilst at Sandhurst he went with Jan Iwandziuk's 1972
expedition to Ethiopia as quartermaster, a task he performed in
the winter of 1973–4 with the Blue Mountains Expedition to
Jamaica. He worked hard on other expeditions to Ethiopia and
Jamaica, which never materialized, and was a last-minute choice
for a minor role in the Zaire River Expedition in 1974–5. He
served with his corps in Germany and at Bicester and led a party
of soldiers on an archaeological expedition to Fast Castle in
Berwickshire in 1976. He was a keen collector and excelled in the
'back-stage' organization of expedition presentations, showing
special skill in the production of visual aids. The British Museum
(Natural History) houses his botanical collection whilst his
entomological specimens are at the Department of Zoology of
Cambridge University. He was not married.

Peter CHADWICK, 28: Cameraman.

Born at Leiston in Suffolk, Peter attended the grammar school
there before going on to study zoology, physics and art at
Ipswich Civic College. But his career was to be in photography
and he took over a London studio as a freelance. His first experience of expedition photography came in Ethiopia in 1972,
where he shot film for Jan Iwandziuk of the prison-palace of
Wehni on its hitherto unclimbed volcanic pinnacle. He next
visited the West Indian island of St Vincent to film parrots,

before joining the British Vulcan Expedition in 1976. He is un-married and lives in Richmond, Surrey.

Major Nicholas (Nick) COOKE, 10th Princess Mary's Own Gurkha Rifles, 41: Expedition Climbing Leader.

Nick's father was successively in the Indian army and the Political Service, and Peshawar, now in Pakistan, was Nick's birthplace. His parents returned to Britain in 1945 and Nick went to Clifton College Prep and then to Dauntsey's in Wiltshire. After a short spell in Southern Rhodesia he returned to work for his family at Bel Royal Vineries in Jersey. In 1954 he entered Eaton Hall and then Sandhurst, after which he was commissioned in the 2nd/10th Gurkhas. For sixteen years he served in the Far East, in anti-terrorist campaigns in Malaya from 1956 to 1959 and in the con-frontation with Indonesia in Borneo from 1963 to 1967. In 1971 he moved into the world of adventure training and became for two years the chief instructor at the Army Outward Bound School at Towyn. From 1973 to 1975 he was commandant of the Army Mountain Training Centre for the BAOR at Silberhütte in the Harz Mountains. During this time he went on skis over the famous Alpine High Level Route and ski-mountaineering became a first love. Before going to Ecuador he was appointed commandant of the Joint-Services Adventure Training Centre in Cyprus. At an investiture in October 1977, he received the George Medal from HM the Queen. Nick and his wife Maxine have two sons, Jason and Roland.

Captain Janusz IWANDZIUK, RE, 25: Expedition Leader.

Jan's parents came from Poland in World War Two, and he was born at Penley, North Wales. Educated in the Potteries at St Joseph's College, Trent Vale, he shone at athletics as a hurdler, long jumper and triple jumper. He went from Newcastle-under-Lyme to university at Newcastle-upon-Tyne, but before com-pleting his degree course he left to join the army. At Sandhurst from 1970 to 1972 he was the first officer-cadet to lead a major expedition – some twenty strong – to Ethiopia. Service in the Royal Engineers took him first to Chatham then to Cyprus, where he helped to rebuild Nicosia Airport after the Turkish invasion of 1974. From Cyprus he returned to the RE Junior

Leaders Regiment in Dover. He married Sarah Wade in February 1976.

Ronald MACE, 28: Cameraman.

Ron was born at Epping and attended the Sir George Monoux Grammar School at Walthamstow between 1964 and 1967. He studied for a further year at Waltham Forest College before moving to the New York Institute of Photography. From 1968 to 1970 he was in the USA. He returned to the London College of Printing but left to go with Jan Iwandziuk on the Sandhurst expedition of 1972 to Ethiopia, where he specialized in sound recording the film. He subsequently worked with the Motor Agents Association and Filmatic Film Laboratories. His American wife, Jeannine, now lives with their daughter, Chelsea, in Walthamstow.

Richard SNAILHAM, MA, FRGS, 46: Expedition writer and interpreter.

Born at Clitheroe in Lancashire, his parents soon moved to Sheffield where he attended Westbourne Preparatory School until 1943. He was further educated at Oakham School and Keble College, Oxford, where he read Modern History. He taught at Alleyn Court School on the Essex coast, at Clayesmore School in Dorset and at Exeter School until becoming, in 1965, a Senior Lecturer at the Royal Military Academy, Sandhurst. His interest in travel has taken him on expeditions to the Middle East, Ethiopia, Zaire, Jamaica and Ecuador, and in 1969 he helped John Blashford-Snell to found the Scientific Exploration Society and became its first Honorary Secretary. One of his six visits to Ethiopia was with a Winston Churchill Memorial Fellowship in 1971, another two years later to take a Serenissima party of tourists along the Historic Route. He was a semi-finalist in BBC TV's 'Mastermind' in 1973 and again on Radio 4's 'Brain of Britain' in 1976. He has written three books, and gives lectures widely on his expedition experiences.

I

Voice of the Andes

Oddly enough, I did not have the same dread of the possibility of disaster when we were preparing to climb Sangay as I had felt in the lower reaches of the Zaire River, when the inflatables were drawing nearer the big rapids at Kinshasa. I suppose it was because others had been up Sangay before.

author in reply to small boy at a lecture who asked,
'Were you afraid of going up an active volcano?'

With a hypodermic syringe in one hand and a swab of cotton wool in the other a little Ecuadorean nurse came brightly into my tiny hospital room.

'*Inyección,*' she said, and I peeled back the blankets and rolled over as far as my shattered right arm would allow. The needle sank easily into my upper leg and in seconds she was gone. Yet another shot of garamicine was quickly absorbed into my bloodstream. The business of being injected had already become an involuntary reflex action and a familiar part of a busy daily routine.

My waking hours were rhythmically punctuated by visits from friends, doctors' rounds, the attentions of a garrulous cleaning lady, a succession of vast meals and the ensuing exercise of natural functions – always a somewhat tense situation, this, as you will understand if you have ever tried asking for a bed-pan in Spanish. Even sign language seemed somehow inadequate here.

The Vozandes Hospital in Quito is linked with a large, evangelical radio station – 'The Voice of the Andes' – run by American missionaries and listened to throughout South

America. Messages of hope are beamed out under the call sign HCJB ('Heralding Christ Jesus's Blessings') from a complex of buildings on one side of the Calle Villalengua in Iñaquito, a northern suburb of the modern part of the city. On the other side of the tree-lined street stands the three-storeyed hospital where two of the British Vulcan Expedition reconnaissance team now lay – myself, with head to window, looking through an open door across a corridor to a similar room which the authorities had thoughtfully given to Peter Chadwick, our cinephoto-grapher. We could communicate easily through a passing stream of shuffling patients, brisk American sisters, priests and policemen.

The policemen were an odd intrusion. Many of the patients, as in all countries, were victims of traffic pile-ups, and after these *accidentes de transito* the drivers involved were guarded by traffic police stationed on the ward. The fear was that when he had recovered sufficiently a guilty party might slip out in his pyjamas and high-tail it homewards. Bored to distraction, the poor policeman, immaculate in his close-fitting, American-style helmet and uniform, with plastic white belt and sling, would from time to time come and sit in our rooms and talk desultorily. A modern, technological marvel such as my tape-recorder exerted a powerful attraction. With a flash of golden teeth he would pick it up and happily beguile a half-hour pressing buttons and listening to our strange English voices.

On other occasions a head, bearded as my own, would appear round the door. 'Hi, Richard! How's it going?'

This was Ronald Cline, one of the HCJB staff, a strongly muscled, good-looking missionary who often called on me. After several minutes' general chat he would say, 'I wonder, Richard, if you'd like it if we prayed together for a while?' Almost all the American missionaries concluded their visits in this way. I do not think I have ever been so intensively prayed over.

Between callers I lay back on my buttress of pillows and stared up at the room's only decoration – a framed, pokerwork text on the wall to my left: '*Venid a mi*', it ran, '*todos los que estais trabajadas y cargados y yo os hare descansar – Mateo, 11.28*'.

The Spanish I had learned at the University of Liverpool's Summer School at San Sebastián in 1951 was the shaky foundation for one of my roles in the reconnaissance team, that of interpreter. I had reinforced it slightly by brief visits to Spain in 1961 and 1970, but my main work of preparation had been done during the flight out to Ecuador on 1 August when I had steeped myself in a paperback, *Spanish through Pictures*. As I disembarked at Quito I had felt like a subscriber to one of those 'You-can-speak-Urdu-after-twelve-hours' advertisements.

But I had probably learned far more by struggling with the language itself in the three weeks that we had now been in Ecuador, and so I had little difficulty with even the archaic, biblical Spanish of this text – 'Come unto me all ye that labour and are heavy laden, and I will give you rest' – familiar as it was, and strangely comforting.

Not normally much of a reader of the New Testament I spent many quiet moments with a copy that the hospital's Catholic chaplain had put in my room. It kept my Spanish up, and my spirits, too.

But for fillips to my morale I did not rely solely on the intercessions of my American friends nor on the written word. In the bedside table cupboard was a bottle of Ecuadorean gin, bought in a supermarket before our journey to the volcano and now a vital part of my life-support system.

Another regular visitor was a jolly, round Ecuadorean lady (most Ecuadorean ladies seemed to be round and jolly), an orderly who replenished patients' soft drinks supplies. '*Jugo!*' she would announce, slamming down a flask of orange juice. I doubt if she knew how valuable her *jugo* was, as I left-handedly decanted a dash of it into the gin in my tooth mug.

Ahead of me I could generally see the silhouette of Peter's tousled head against the window behind him and the occasional glint of light on his glasses. He, too, had a broken right arm and so sat upright most of the time. Now his face was contorted and his head shaking up and down. Peter has a fiendish stammer and so I realized he was simply trying to say something. I waited until he had got up a sufficient head of steam.

'Wonder what's for lunch?' he shouted, somewhat anticlimactically.

'Almost bound to be rice,' I said.

His head shuddered again.

'Like living in Hong Kong!'

'Or Gerrard Street!'

Sure enough it would be rice, sometimes with meat, sometimes with *corvina*, an excellent fish from the Pacific. And preceded by a bowl of soup with a knuckle of bone floating in it. We were both finding it a sticky business getting it all into the mouth with our less adept hand.

'My mother once went round Chartwell,' I told Peter, 'and got into conversation with an old member of the staff who also happened to come from Yorkshire. "Ee, that Churchill," she said, "'e were a messy eater!" Gem of history for you!'

Sometimes the endless rice palled.

'I could do with a carefully done *Tournedos rossini*,' I said.

Peter shook again. 'They ought to do *Croque monsieur* for us two.'

Early on in our nine days in the Vozandes we had both had operations. This involved the usual shaving of the affected parts, donning of a flimsy nightshirt and pre-med injections. Then at intervals of a few hours we were wheeled away to the lift. I did not sing 'We're off to see the wizard, the wonderful wizard of Oz!' as I had done once in a Bournemouth hospital, but was nonetheless very cheerful. From the lift the wheel-chair propelled me into a small room with an operating table in the centre and some lights above. Surgical equipment stood in every corner and shelves stacked with bandages and dressings covered the four walls. It was a sort of Aladdin's cave.

All around were figures in green gowns. I recognized

Dr Guillermo Guerra, the surgeon, who was sorting out his scalpels.

'Good morning, Mr Snailham. And how are *you* today?' came from behind his mask.

I greeted him, and the anaesthetist who had visited me the previous evening, and nodded at the assemblage of nurses. Above the muttered conversations came the clink of instruments and the squeak and snap of rubber gloves. It was all very informal and matey.

'Would you mind getting on to the table please?' said Dr Guerra.

I rose from the wheel-chair, hoisted myself awkwardly up, lay down, stretched my left arm out towards the anaesthetist and soon sank into the arms of Lethe.

I suppose it was natural that I should dream of England and of where I live and work. I seemed to see Clifford Pierce, my old servant at Sandhurst, standing over me. He appeared to be saying something, but I could not tell what. It might have been 'Nasty ole mornin', sir', or 'I took your suit to the . . . er, wossname, like you said.' Was he holding out a cup of that curious beverage which the army dishes up to its officers as morning tea? But no, it was a dark brown hand that the equally tall Dr Guerra stretched out to me, and I was back in my little room on the third floor.

As I swam back up to consciousness I realized that I was effectively trapped: a saline drip was fixed into a blood-vessel in my left arm and an antibiotic drip passed through a hole in the plaster that now encased my right arm and out again to a sort of vacuum-operated sump on the floor.

'No dodging away from the *policía* now,' I said to Peter, who was similarly hooked up.

It was a time for reflection. My dominant emotion was one of relief. Six of us had set off up the mountain, two were now dead. I had survived odds of one in three. To have received compound, comminuted fractures above and below the elbow seemed a small price to pay. I was confident now that my arm would be saved. The cocoon-like warmth of my hospital bed, the security of my private room, the support of so many friends all contributed to my sense of well-being. But what of these others?

The most frequent visitor we had was Peter Francis, whom I hardly knew at the outset but who soon became a firm friend. Dr Francis was the well-spring of the whole expedition. Pale and wiry, his outwardly intense, serious manner belying a capacity for quiet humour, he is a young lecturer in earth sciences in the Open University at Milton Keynes. A specialist in volcanoes, he had guided the expedition through its preparatory phase, conferring with our leadership in a series of meetings in London pubs and at the premises of the Royal Geographical Society. A week before the departure of the reconnaissance team Penguin Books had brought out his *Volcanoes*, a definitive work on the subject. Sadly, though, obligations to the Open University precluded his being with us on the flight out and so he would miss the first of our three climbs. A fortnight later he was coming out to join the reconnaissance when the public address system at Charles de Gaulle airport informed him of the Sangay tragedy. Considerately he had continued his journey and was now proving most helpful in the grisly administrative aftermath, as well as being most solicitous of the welfare of the wounded.

'I thought you might like this,' he said, putting a copy of *All the President's Men* on my cupboard top. 'Compulsive reading.'

'I hope I'll have time for it,' I said, glancing at the stack of literature I had already accumulated. Reading in hospital is never as easy as might be supposed: halfway through some poignant paragraph in comes a nurse to take a pulse or administer a blanket bath.

'How's Jan?' I asked.

Jan Iwandziuk, our leader, was the most gravely wounded survivor and was in the Andrade Marín Hospital, a big establishment which specializes in complex cases and has an intensive care unit. Jan, a tall, fair Royal Engineers captain, was just about to undergo delicate brain surgery there.

'He'll be all right,' said Peter Francis. 'Herbert Reyes is

reckoned to be one of the best head men in South America.'

'Not a Jivaro, is he?'

Peter ignored this unworthy flippancy.

'Gave me great confidence when we met him yesterday. Trained in the States. And the firm Sarah works for have paid for her to come out in a day or two's time.'

Sarah was Jan's wife, and I had been an usher at their wedding in Henley-on-Thames only six months previously. Best man on that chilly St Valentine's Day occasion had been Lieutenant Adrian Ashby-Smith, RAOC, Jan's dear friend from their Sandhurst days together, and mine through three earlier expeditions. He was quartermaster to the reconnaissance team, and he had died on Sangay.

Ronald Mace, stills photographer, had also perished on the mountain. A chubby, laconic Essex man, he had assisted Peter Chadwick to make a film of Jan Iwandziuk's first expedition that, whilst still an officer-cadet at the Royal Military Academy, Jan had led to Ethiopia. I had accompanied them on this venture, in the summer of 1972, and it was here that Adrian Ashby-Smith also had first practised his quartermastering skills. So five of us shared common expedition experiences, and we had been from the start a fairly well-knit team whose compatability was more or less proven.

'Nick's at home,' Peter Francis went on, 'resting his sore head.' The only member of the climbing team not previously known to all the others was Nick Cooke, a major in the 10th Gurkha Rifles and at this time the commandant of the Joint Services Adventure Training Centre in Cyprus. Nick had been in the Vozandes hospital briefly while his head of wispy, fair hair was partially shaved and then roughly scoured to cleanse it of embedded bits of volcanic ash and grit. He, like Peter Francis, was now a regular visitor to our ward and had brought me, *inter alia*, a vast slab of Ecuadorean chocolate.

'He's beginning to chafe a bit,' said Peter. 'Wants to get back to his wife and kids in Cyprus, but Peter Wills is not too keen to let him go.'

'Well, it's surely true that there's a lot for him to sort out here,' I added.

Group-Captain Peter Wills was defence attaché at the British Embassy in Quito. A tall, distinguished-looking RAF officer of long experience, with a keen scientific mind and a generous heart, he had reacted rather nervously to our arrival. However, we put this down to the fact that in early August, with his ambassador on leave, he was faced with the conjunction of *three* British expeditions in his one small parish:t he army's Scottish Command Los Tayos Expedition was still in the field, and a Cambridge University agricultural survey team arrived in Ecuador just about when we did.

Not only had Peter Wills master-minded our rescue from the volcano, but his spacious suburban house was now the reconnaissance team's focal point, and he and his Canadian wife, Dorothy, were our main source of support and comfort. Nick Cooke was living with them and they, too, with their son Simon who was on holiday from Sherborne, came to the Vozandes almost daily. When I once asked for a handkerchief Dorothy cut out and hem-stitched some for me, and Peter Chadwick and I, unable yet to grasp pens in our writing hands, dictated postcards to her and Simon. The Wills family and many of the embassy staff, both in their official roles and privately, were unstinting in their care for us.

So there were no *longueurs* for Chadwick and me as we lay, variously pinioned in plaster of paris and hooked up beneath pendulous cylinders of high-octane life-restorer. People came and went with gossip, mail, books, flagons of fruit juice and even clippings from the British press.

There's no news like bad news and from the moment of the disaster we had been widely featured by the media in Ecuador, the United States and Britain. Reporters penetrated the hospital and even before my operation (but after the pre-med injection) I gave a carefree and probably unintelligible interview, entirely in Spanish, to an Ecuadorean radio man. Another charming visitor was Tim Ross, *The Observer*'s correspondent in Latin America, who was later to do something of a hatchet job on our reconnaissance efforts. Naturally enough, we recorded a piece for HCJB, and Nick Cooke, in the Wills's house, was already getting importunate phone calls from representatives of the British national dailies in New York and Florida. The fruits of these were to have serious repercussions later.

The story had filled a page and a half in one of the local papers, *El Comercio*, on 18 August, the day after our rescue: *'Con dos víctimas concluyó drama de Ingleses en Sangay'* the headlines ran. A copy lay on my bedside table, and I saw that it not only styled me *'el profesor Richard Snailhan'* but further on, *'el profesor de Geología de la Academia inglesa de Sandhurst'*. Many British papers were to take up this gem of misinformation which would, I felt, give some amusement at the RMAS where I was merely one of many senior lecturers and where geology had probably never been taught. Army officers were supposed to be good judges of ground but not to the extent of knowing how the landscape was formed and what made it up. Would it enhance an exercise, I mused, to tell officer-cadets that they were digging their fox-holes in red breccia and marl or constructing their sangars of carboniferous limestone, 'and notice the interesting veins of quartz'? I could imagine a few dark looks being exchanged as the 'professor of Geology' went on his way to the mess tent.

My work at Sandhurst was in the field of modern history, but it was quite understandable on a primarily geological expedition that I should be labelled a geologist.

Lying underneath *El Comercio* were some coloured glossies from the *Dirección Nacional de Turismo*. There was one called *Ecuador: Paraíso del Turista*. With my good hand I flicked through it and tried to feel like a tourist.

2
Fire in their Bellies

In Ecuador there are about fifty volcanoes of which nine
[have] had eruptions in historical time. . . . The most active
ones at present are Sangay and Reventador.

M. Neumann Van Padang, *Catalogue of the
Active Volcanoes of the World*

'We are travellers, you are tourists, they are trippers. . . .' I
have always been inclined to go along with this snobbish
little axiom and have tried to avoid going anywhere as a
tourist pure and simple. Much more satisfying to aspire to
be a traveller, I have felt.

An expedition falls firmly into the category of travel and
most of my journeying in the world has so far been by this
means. But how did I come to be involved with this
particular venture to Ecuador?

The expedition was first conceived in the early 1970s
when Peter Francis, keen to do some more volcanological
field-work in the Andes (his studies had already carried him
to Chile, Bolivia, Peru, Ecuador and Colombia, as well as to
Central America and the Tyrrhenian Sea), approached
Lieutenant-Colonel David Hall, RE, who is chairman of
the Royal Engineers Mountaineering and Exploration
Society. Tall, dark-moustached and militarily correct in
dress and manner, David Hall is – dare one say it? – the
second best-known sapper Lieutenant-Colonel in the exploring business. Unlike the more flamboyant John Blashford-
Snell, David Hall has made a niche for himself as a specialist
(in desert navigation) and has close links with the Royal

Geographical Society, where he occupies the splendidly titled position of honorary foreign secretary.

The sort of combination between scientists and military that Peter Francis had in mind is one for which the Scientific Exploration Society, since its formation in 1969, has become well known. The geologists would say where they wanted to go, and the army would get them there and back again.

Casting around for a leader, Hall first selected SES member Captain Harley Nott, RE, who had led in 1973-4 a similar, successful venture to the Blue Mountains of Jamaica.

The first Andean volcano sites that Francis lighted on were not in Ecuador but in Chile, but in the event, the exigencies of the service determined that Nott could not make it, and Chile's revolution of 1974, in which Pinochet ousted Allende, meant that that country became for the time being politically off-limits. So it came about that fellow-sapper Jan Iwandziuk was asked to take over the leadership and stable, right-wing Ecuador became the new venue for the volcanological enquiries.

The selection of expedition sites from the point of view of their political viability is a mystery worthy of specialist study in itself. In fact, it remains one of the trickiest imponderables of expedition planning. David Hall had had his own hard experience of it when a carefully constructed desert expedition to the Tibesti region of southern Libya was rudely aborted by Colonel Qadaffi's deposition of King Idris in 1969. David was fortunately able to re-route his whole enterprise to the Aïr Mountains of neighbouring Niger and successfully carry out a full scientific programme there.

Now Chile had undergone revolution. It had swung violently from left to right, which ostensibly would seem to make it *more* attractive to the authorities in Britain. But it had gone *too far* right and was being branded as fascist. Questions were asked in the House of Commons when the Scottish soccer team proposed to play in Santiago in 1977, and so it would never have done for even a quasi-official scientific expedition to go there.* Ecuador also had a right-wing government, vested in a three-man junta of its service chiefs, but it was decently right-wing: no unpleasant news of torturings reached the world's headlines, no earnest student resolutions sought to empty its jails of communists, and so it would do.

I had known of these developments for some months and had had many a long telephone discussion with Jan Iwand-ziuk about them. During one such call Jan asked, 'How would you like to come along with us and write about it? Are you free?'

'My dear Jan,' I said, 'I'm freedom's prisoner.'

My motives were mixed. In part, there was the straight-forward lure of Ecuador – a new country for me, indeed a new continent. A quaint, small land, off the beaten track. Perhaps a kind of South American Ethiopia (an old love of mine) – both mountain lands with high-altitude capitals, full of character; both flanked by tropical rain forests and low-lying coastal plains ('And they both begin with E,' added Jan helpfully). Then there was the prospect of going on another venture with old friends – Jan himself, and possibly Adrian Ashby-Smith, Peter Chadwick and Ron Mace. Expedition history never repeats itself any more than the history of any other undertaking, yet I felt that this cast list offered good chances of another rewarding, amusing experience.

Furthermore, I had for the past five years been deeply involved with the vast, prestigious, widely publicized Zaire River Expedition and had just finished writing the author-ized book about it. It was the second time I had written of hazardous exploits on famous rivers, and now I felt I needed a change of theme. Agreeing the final version of the story of ZRE had been a taxing, time-consuming and frequently bitter business. I needed a rest from its com-plexities. I was disenchanted, as John Blashford-Snell him-

---

* There was some military involvement, and weighty institutions like the Royal Society and the Royal Geographical Society were connected with it.

self had temporarily been, with big, blockbuster expeditions and felt that a six- or seven-man venture to Ecuador might recapture for me the purer, quintessential delights of expeditioneering. John himself, after ZRE, went off on a similarly escapist, family jaunt to Nepal. And his next expedition had been a small reconnaissance affair to Caledonia Bay in Panama.

So, for a multiplicity of reasons, I was to be writer and interpreter for the British Vulcan Expedition reconnaissance, which was finally scheduled to work in Ecuador for six weeks in August and September of 1976.

Few expeditions have untroubled approaches to the runway, and take-off is often delayed. Indeed the timing is almost as much of an imponderable as the siting of them. In common with many previous SES ventures our Ecuadorean project had a chequered preparatory phase.* Almost at its culmination there were moves to stall it further, but there comes a point when involvement has become so deep that to apply the brakes with the tail-wheel already off the ground would be as damaging for an expedition as for an aircraft.

So with the minimum of pre-expedition gatherings and with doubts and obfuscations in a number of areas we made ready for 1 August. Peter Francis was handsomely backed by a grant from the Royal Society. He and Jan Iwandziuk also secured financial support from the Royal Geographical Society and the Mount Everest Foundation.

Camp equipment and climbing gear was borrowed from various military sources and from the Scientific Exploration Society, an altimeter came from the Open University and the usual consumer goods from the usual commercial sponsors. Quietly, almost surreptitiously, Adrian Ashby-Smith proceeded with his work as quartermaster, garnering and docketing all these items.

* The Blue Nile Expedition of 1968 was nearly extinguished by Foreign Office pressures. Harley Nott's Blue Mountains Expedition to Jamaica was four times postponed and even ZRE was an uncertain starter eight months before it left.

It happened quietly because Adrian was for some reason under something of a professional cloud. His presence on the expedition list was not acceptable in some quarters. On the Zaire River Expedition his performance had been patchy, and John Blashford-Snell, chairman of the Scientific Exploration Society and a powerful weight in army adventure training circles, did not think at all highly of him. Worse, there was opposition to Adrian from some other army top brass who seemed to want him permanently blacked from expeditions. Jan Iwandziuk, however, rated him the best small expedition quartermaster he knew, and in this field I, too, felt he had no equals. Though an unconventional young officer with a scant regard for traditional standards of dress, he was loyal and selfless to a fault and a dedicated expedition man. Aside from the tedious business of looking after all the kit he always found time for zoological and botanical collecting work and was a true lover of nature and wild places. Jan had listed him as deputy leader and desperately wanted to give Adrian this chance to prove himself. Somehow he hoped to circumvent official objections.

Who else was actually to go? Question marks hung over other potential reconnaissance team members besides Adrian. Those finally listed were three: Nick Cooke, Adrian Ashby-Smith and Jan himself, though Adrian was a doubtful participant right up to the last.

There were others, including myself, who knew that they were in the team but were not listed. This was the result of a divergence of views between Peter Francis and Jan. Peter had unequivocally made it clear at an early stage that he did not want the reconnaissance to include a film crew. It would be a distracting, time-wasting encumbrance, he felt, and would weaken the scientific resolve of the team. He had assured the Royal Society that there were no such supernumeraries, and when pressed by Jan he had compromised only to the extent of allowing one cine-camera to be taken to record scientific finds.

Jan, on the other hand, knew from past experience that

good photographic stills and a few thousand feet of show-able film are often a great help in eliciting further support from commerce, industry and the general public. And the expedition which would follow the reconnaissance, timed tentatively for the summer of 1977, would need a great deal more money. Two or three illustrated presentations, after the reconnaissance, would surely help to bring it in.

In addition, Jan's first soundings of Ron Mace and Peter Chadwick, film-makers to his Sandhurst Ethiopian Expedition of 1972, had met with a ready response. Ron in particular was most eager to go to Ecuador and threw himself into the preparations with great vigour.

Thus Jan found himself in a dilemma: Peter Francis was obdurate about film-making, whilst Ron Mace, in Waltham-stow, was beavering away at procuring film and making travel arrangements.

Jan's parents had come from Poland during World War Two, his father escaping from captivity in Russia and join-ing the Allied forces via the Middle East. Jan inherited a dogged determination, found often among the slav peoples; it is not in his nature to buckle under difficulties. He inwardly hoped it would be possible to include a small film team and thought that later on he could reconcile this difference between himself and Peter. But the situation might, for the moment, call for a bit of subterfuge.

A useful element of *fait accompli* could be achieved, he thought, by having the film team leave Britain earlier than the rest of us and by a different route. Initial detachment might soften the blow of our eventual reunion and make it seem, in a sense, accidental. So I was asked to get Mace and Chadwick out to Ecuador by ship, which would not only separate us but be a considerable saving in costly air fares. The kind cooperation of Captain Murray and the Pacific Steam Navigation Company of Liverpool secured us two free berths on MV *Orcoma*, sailing for Guayaquil on 14 July.

Meanwhile, team members leafed through the printed prospectus that Jan had produced. But Ecuador still felt

very far away and unreal. The three volcanoes that concerned us – Sangay, Sumaco and Reventador – were just
crosses in large, white, open spaces on the map. The nearest
town to Sangay (which we learnt to pronounce 'Sang'-gī')
was Riobamba, which I thought had a suitably South
American ring about it. It probably relapsed into carnival
about every ten days, I imagined, when proud girls with
narrow eyes and high Inca cheekbones – all looking like
descendants of Atahualpa – would swirl and dance in the
broad, dusty plaza (dancing the riobamba, perhaps?) while
donkeys ruminated in the shade and the men slept under
those gigantic sombreros.

But the prospectus was business-like enough:

EXPEDITION AIMS

Both Sangay and Sumaco lie in areas which are poorly mapped
(if at all) both topographically and geologically. They lie in areas
termed inaccessible by official sources. The expedition will carry
out a scientific programme of study and exploration, including
topographical and geological mapping in those areas. . . .

During a scientific visit in May 1975, a party from the Escuela
Politécnica Nacional, Quito, did not reach the summit vents of
Sangay due to conditions at that time on the summit. With
careful planning and preparation this expedition intends to reach
the summit and collect gas samples from within the vent, together
with geological samples. . . .

From Quito the expedition will move south beyond Riobamba,
and then strike south-east on a four-day cross-country march
with mules to Sangay, an active volcano, approximate position
02°02'S, 78°20'W. No gas sample specimens from this type of
volcano exist, and great interest has been expressed in their
collection. The problem of collecting the samples is getting close
enough to the vent hole to take a pure sample. Also the volcano
rises to over 17000 ft and getting to the crater rim presents a
challenge in itself. . . .

Of course, our reconnaissance would not be collecting
gases or making maps. This was for the expedition proper.
Our job was to pave the way, to make the necessary local

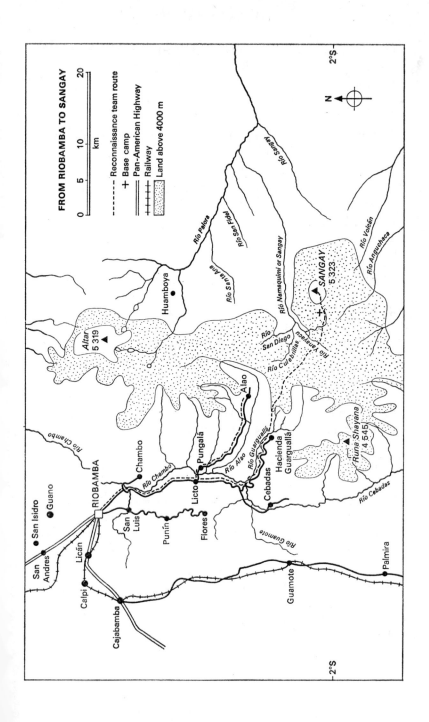

FROM RIOBAMBA TO SANGAY

- - - - Reconnaissance team route
+ Base camp
Pan-American Highway
⊦⊦⊦⊦ Railway
Land above 4000 m

0   5   10   20
km

N

2°S

Río Chambo
San Isidro
Guano
San Andrés
Licán
Calpi
Cajabamba
RIOBAMBA
San Luis
Punín
Flores
Chambo
Río Chambo
Licto
Pungalá
Río Alao
Río Guarguallá
Alao
Cebadas
Hacienda Guarguallá
'Runa Shavana' 4 545
Río Cebadas
Río Guamote
Guamote
Palmira
Altar 5 319
Huamboya
Río Palora
Río San Fidel
Río Santa Ana
Río San
Río Namequimi or Sangay
Río San Diego
Río Culebrillas
Río Yanayacu
SANGAY 5 323
+
Río Volcán
Río Anguchaca
Río Sangay

2°S

contacts, to assess the logistic problems involved in leading a party of scientists to the summits of three volcanoes, and to report on these problems.

For Sangay we had specific questions to answer:

1. Difficulty of ascent; duration of ascent; feasibility of carriage of scientific equipment to summit.
2. Practicability of camp-site near summit; necessity for level site (on ice, snow or lava?); direction of prevailing wind, strength of fumes, safe distance; direction of fall of ash, distance.
3. Shape, diameter, depth of crater(s); number of vents; type of vent and activity prevailing (gas? ash?); possibility of descent into crater(s); frequency of activity and pattern, if any.
4. Distribution and nature of parasitic vents; accessibility to vents, nature of activity.
5. Nature and distribution of pyroclastic deposits around volcano.
6. Consultation with geologists and local population (if any) on recent activity and type.
7. Feasibility of making plane table survey.
8. Design of surveying programme.

The high seriousness of our purpose was dented slightly by facetious friends who towards departure time would say helpful things like, 'Hope it all goes like a bomb – the expedition, I mean,' and 'Don't forget your smoking jacket,' or ask interesting questions like, 'What happens when you are climbing up the snow and it suddenly ends and it's just rocks and ashes which get hotter and hotter? Will you pull asbestos boots out of your rucksacks, slip into something fireproof and just carry on?'

Like previous climbers of Sangay we would have to play that one by ear.

3
To the Road's End

You spend your boyhood dreaming of a magic, impossibly distant day when you will cross the Equator, when your eyes will behold Quito. And then, in the slow prosaic process of life, that day undramatically dawns. . . .

Christopher Isherwood, *The Condor and the Cows*

Accelerating their preparations, Peter Chadwick and Ron Mace took a hired car to Liverpool and boarded the neat M V *Orcoma* in Huskisson Dock. A good deal of expedition kit went aboard with them, and they slipped from the Mersey on 14 July.

Ron and Peter were to work as deck-hands during the three-week voyage to Guayaquil. They had a very merry, not too arduous time. We received a wish-you-were-here postcard from Bermuda, some old paint was indeed chipped from the *Orcoma*'s buff funnel, but Peter spent most of his time shooting the ship and its complement in action, with the intention that a short publicity film should ultimately be given to the Pacific Steam Navigation Company in return for their generosity.

Now part of the Furness Withy Group, this company was founded by an American, William Wheelwright, and given a Royal Charter in 1840. It has since specialized in trade between Britain and the west coast of South America, first via the Magellan Straits and after 1914 through the Panama Canal. The line's third ship, a 323-ton iron paddle steamer launched at Glasgow in 1845, was called *Ecuador*. By the 1870s the PSNC had become the largest steamship under-

taking in the world with fifty-seven vessels. Their first
Orcoma was a twin-screw ship of the early 1900s lavishly
equipped with electrically powered devices. The passenger
service has ended now but the company still operates seven
cargo vessels and the 14848-ton *Orcoma* that Ron and Peter
travelled on was built in 1966 and runs regularly between
Liverpool and San Antonio, Chile.

Most of its ports of call are considered by the PSNC to
be too hazardous for their ship's crews to be allowed
ashore, so places like Kingston, Jamaica, were not visited.
But a pleasant day was spent exploring the walls and
bastions of the old Spanish city of Cartagena in Colombia.
The Panama Canal, sadly for Peter's film, was passed at
night.

But they were still driving steadily across the Pacific on
1 August when a small knot of other team members
gathered at Heathrow – Jan, Nick, Adrian and myself. Ron
Mace had arranged flights the cheapest way possible, and
this turned out to be by British Airways to Madrid, thence
by Aerovias Quisqueyana to Miami (via Santo Domingo),
and by Ecuatoriana to Quito (via Nassau and Bogotá).
Tracing these last two airlines involved quite a deal of
research.

'What do you make of it?' asked Jan.

'*Quisque* is the Latin for "whoever",' I suggested rather
tamely.

'Oh, well, it means, "Whoever would go by this airline?"'
said Nick.

It turned out that Aerovias Quisqueyana was the national
airline of the Dominican Republic.

The Isle of Wight, parched by months of drought,
looked more like Morocco. Soon we were over the Coten-
tin, La Baule, the Bay of Biscay and Spain. At Madrid we
entered the first of several of those states of limbo, where
travellers lounge about listlessly, too jet-lagged even to
read, or wander, untempted, among those garish souvenir
stalls which are cheap and expensive at one and the same
time.

But from the windows of this limbo we could see a white Boeing 707 unmistakably marked AEROVIAS QUISQUE-YANA in red, so escape was possible. As this airline was not a member of IATA we experienced some special problems, however: no check-in desk; worse still, no mention of our flight on the public address system, or on the overhead indicator boards as they riffled through their departure schedules. By some mysterious telepathic process a group of passengers, all more or less Latin-American looking, were corralled together like errant sheep by a swarthy official, and we followed them out to a waiting bus.

After an agonizingly long take-off, our transatlantic stage was not as bad as had been anticipated. The Dominican stewardesses giggled in the galley but eventually produced food and drink. I put my watch back six hours as we headed into an interminable sunset, not quite keeping up with the tomato-coloured orb but at least delaying its descent.

Some passengers became apprehensive as we entered a violent electrical storm over Santo Domingo, but the plane, which had seen some service – its seat belts were marked PAN AM and the notices over the exits were in Turkish – was brought down neatly enough.

After a tedious wait in the Aeropuerta Internacional de los Americas with its brightly lit but almost wholly unpatron-ized duty-free shop, we flew on wearily to Miami. Here there was a hiccup – our onward flight by an Ecuadorean plane to Quito was over-booked. So, in accordance with airline practice we were taken to an hotel – a nearby, lofty matchbox called the Ramada Inn.

Miami was huge and humid and most of it lay between the airport and the sea. We left the hotel only to walk round the block opposite (which was a hire-car parking lot) or take a dip in the pool under the hot sun. Indoors was air-conditioned darkness and a mock-medieval décor in moulded plastic, with phoney suits of armour, maces and chains. In the Crown and Sceptre Room bar-girls wore micro-dresses, frilly white pants, loosely laced-up bodices and floppy black hats with white plumes like a Hals cavalier. The high Andes seemed a world away.

Next evening we were back in the Miami airport limbo. After turkey sandwiches and ice-cream we slumped and dozed. Air travel was becoming an accepted way of life – hand-baggage inspections, dreary duty-free emporia, piped muzak and burly security spooks.

The final leg was appropriately exotic. We were welcomed aboard Ecuatoriana's Boeing 707 *Imbabura* by no fewer than ten beautiful stewardesses, each in her majestic pale-blue Inca hat (like a giant, inverted cooling tower) and high-collared blue dress. The exterior of the plane, I had noticed, was as striking and bizarre as its stewardesses. No traditional monochrome for Ecuatoriana – the entire fuselage was picked out in bright yellow, blue, red and black blobs and whirls as if a classroom of kids had been turned loose on it. Idly glancing at the safety instructions, I noted that they made special provisions for *personas obesas*. After all this airline and hotel food it seemed specially relevant.

We crossed the first Andes in cloud, but as we dropped over into the southern hemisphere we were above an arid landscape. The plane gyrated sharply from right to left. We were losing height in a confined space and soon dropped onto the tarmac at Quito. Its international airport has a tricky approach from the north and British Airways, for one, does not use it. Adrenalin pumped as it usually did when I stepped out into a new country, on a new venture. The sun was bright, the air had a freshness in it at 9500 feet. It seemed just like the 'perpetual springtime' that the guide books had written about. I felt good.

Entry to Ecuador was simplicity itself: no visa requirement, no customs inspection, no health checks, just 'How long would you like to stay, *señor*?' We settled on forty days. The taxi drive to the British Embassy gave us some first impressions of the capital. The flanks of a dormant volcano, Pichincha, loom over the city to the west, and on the other side are low hills beyond which the ground falls away sharply to a valley bottom with the eastern arm of the

Andean cordillera in the far haze. Quito lies on a long, narrow shelf and can expand only to north and south.

'Is a big city,' I said to the taxi-driver, knowing really that it wasn't, but being conversational.

'No, es pequeño,' he said truthfully, 'but it is long drawn out.'

Past the bull-ring, past the football stadium and up to the Hotel Quito (an Inter-Continental). Opposite, in a non-descript office block, was our embassy, and next door (how difficult it is ever to get away!) was a squat house called El Pub Inglés.

Our link man in the embassy was the defence attaché, Peter Wills, and Jan Iwandziuk went in straight away to confer with him, while the rest of us took turns to go over the road to the *caballeros* in the Hotel Quito for a wash and a shave. Peter Wills, the doyen of the defence attachés after his four years' service in Quito, later met us rather agitatedly on the embassy stairs; nothing was going right for him that day – the security system was being rebuilt and none of the embassy phones was working properly.

However, he had managed to arrange a meeting with our immediate sponsors – a group of British scientists seconded by the Overseas Development Ministry to work with the Ecuadorean Department of Geology and Mines. This British Geological Mission was led by the lean, boyish Dr Brian Kennerley, with whom we had been corresponding for a long time.

He had been most cooperative and could not have been more so now. Not only did he offer us the use of one of the mission's five Land-Rovers for our work on the three volcanoes, but he immediately gave the team temporary accommodation in his own house.

As Brian drove us back towards the football stadium it all seemed to me so much like previous experiences in Addis Ababa, Kingston or Kinshasa. It never fails to impress me how soon and how readily the expatriate community rallies round an incoming expedition and begins to harness local resources on its behalf.

Like most houses in up-town Quito, Brian and Margaret Kennerley's was spacious, wooden-floored and interestingly planned. Quito is an architect's paradise. Whatever he designs is built, and in the smart districts no two places seemed to be the same: arrestingly split levels greeted us, sunken patios and walls of glass giving out onto trim lawns.

A flight of steps led up to Brian's front hall and below was a long basement where he let us sort and store our kit. Adrian Ashby-Smith, barefoot now and in blue denim, began his quiet, patient work of unpacking and centralizing things.

Jan had planned that the reconnaissance should be directed to Sangay first, then Sumaco and Reventador. We had arrived in Quito on the morning of 3 August, and we knew that we had a tight schedule.

'We leave for Riobamba at two p.m. on August 5th,' he now told us. 'That gives us just over two days for preparations here, so we must get our skates on. And I aim to be back here to tackle the other two volcanoes by the night of August 16th.'

So by Land-Rover, taxi or bus the four of us were to be deployed around the city on various errands.

Once we had learnt a few route numbers, buses proved to be the best way of getting about. The city bus was a bulbous, single-decker shoe-box which seemed too big for its wheel-base. There were no set stops but buses could be hailed, preferably at street intersections, and they ambled along picking up and setting down and charging just one sucre (about 2p) for any urban journey.

Finding our way was made complicated by the South American habit of naming streets and squares after historically famous days in their calendars, presumably when a battle had been won or one regime given way to another. In Quito not only was there an Avenida 10 de Agosto, an Avenida 12 de Octubre, an Avenida 6 de Diciembre, but also a 24 de Mayo, an 18 de Septiembre and a 9 de Octubre. Most revolutions seemed to have occurred in the late summer, and I wondered if this was true in other tropical states. When Peter Chadwick later reached Quito, he found this obsession with anniversaries all too much, boarded a bus in the wrong street and spent half a day lost in the suburbs.

Our first and most important call was to the Department of Geology and Mines. Brian, Jan and I were welcomed effusively by its director general, Ingeniero Carlos Mosquera, who listened attentively to our proposals, agreed to collaborate with us and underwrote the loan of a Land-Rover from the *Proyecto Geológico de Gran Bretaña*. He further offered a *chófer* to drive it, a young Ecuadorean geologist to accompany us and 6000 sucres to help pay for petrol, mules and guides. We had made a fortunate start, and I gave Brian my copy of Peter Francis's *Volcanoes* as a small token of thanks.

But with some apprehension we learned from Brian that there were others in the field. Minard L. Hall, an American geologist teaching at the local polytechnic, was currently collecting rocks on Sangay, and the internationally distinguished volcanologist, Haroun Tazieff, had arrived in Quito on the same day as we had, and he planned to take his eight-man team of high-powered scientists in two or three days' time – to Sangay!

Nothing would steal our thunder more effectively than being joined along the way to the same mountain by another – more prestigious – expedition. Haroun Tazieff, traveller, writer, film-maker, had burst upon the world twenty years before by shooting scenes within the throat of Etna for his epic, *Volcano*. At sixty-five he was still among the world's foremost explorers of terrestrial hot-spots. Not only was there already some confusion in Britain as to whether we and the Los Tayos Expedition, who had been exploring caves for some weeks in Oriente province, were one and the same thing. Now we might be overshadowed by another, bigger enterprise setting out with similar objectives. It was infuriating that Sangay had suddenly become so crowded, and this coincidence further spurred Jan on to leave for Riobamba as soon as possible.

First we had to have some maps, so in our last hours we drove to the Instituto Geográfica Militar, high on a rocky hill overlooking the city, and bought a town plan of Quito, air photographs of the approaches to Sangay and Sumaco, and maps of Ecuador.

The 1:100000 scale maps were then only complete for the coastal province of Guayas and the Andean chain from Quito south to the Peruvian border, and the sheet which covers the region south-east of Riobamba towards Sangay maddeningly stops just short of our roadhead destination at Alao. For the fifteen further miles we were to travel with mules and on foot we should have to rely on local guides, on air photographs or the 1:1 million map of the whole country.

Peter Wills took Jan, Nick and me on a courtesy call to the Ecuadorean Ministry of Defence. We left Adrian in his storeroom, as he had already acquired the patina of grime and the dishevelment of dress which was his preferred expedition style. Ecuador's defences are controlled from a complex of faded colonial buildings in the southern part of the city. It was all rather like the stock Latin-American cartoon: braided *coronels* and *mayors* came down flights of steps to climb into *chófer*-driven Impalas, which hooted imperiously as they fought their way out of the crowded car park. Our mission was merely to thank their army for the helpful noises they had made, and to say that we did not need any active aid from them as the Department of Geology and Mines had provided it all. This we conveyed to Mayor de C. Gustavo V. Cañivares E. and with many a '*Muchas gracias!*' we left.

On our final evening, the Kennerleys thoughtfully gave a party at which we met other members of the British community who were to play a key part in the dramas that were to follow: tall, bearded Dr Jeff Aucott, another of the British geological team, and his wife, Pat; Miss Terry Newenham, the ambassador's PA, a blonde but untypical Foreign Office bird, shy, quiet and tirelessly thoughtful; and, rather late from El Pub Inglés, forestry adviser Allan

Miller, an idiosyncratic and popular figure who enters a vintage Rolls-Royce in Ecuadorean car rallies.

Just before we left Quito the next day we drove down into the valley east of the city to Allan Miller's house in the dormitory suburb of Tumbaco to hire crampons, ice-axes, gaiters and other climbing paraphernalia. Allan is secretary of one of Ecuador's numerous climbing clubs, and had himself been in a party which went most of the way up Sangay a year or two before but was beaten back by clouds of molten ash.

We thought we now had a fair mental picture of the volcano (few *actual* pictures exist as the region is almost always heavily clouded) from what we had read and from eye-witnesses like Allan, whom we had eagerly quizzed. We were ready, and raring, to go. I still felt with intensity the excitements of being a new arrival in an unfamiliar, exotic capital whose attractive, historic heart we had yet to see; but other, different excitements beckoned us strongly.

We made our farewells to Margaret Kennerley and gave her an appropriate box of 'El Sangay' tea-bags and five red roses (there should have been one from each of us but the sixth we lost in the bus on the way back). We then collected our Land-Rover from Brian Kennerley at the Department of Geology and Mines. In the event, no *chófer* was assigned to us, but we now met our Ecuadorean geologist, Gerardo Herrera. Tall, slim, moustachioed and with a shock of black, curly hair, he spoke a little, rather excitable English and was to prove a key factor in our eventual escape from Sangay.

At the eleventh hour before going into the field occurred one of those little official difficulties with which experience has made me familiar. We had parked our Land-Rover outside the embassy and were going inside to announce our departure and thank Peter Wills and Terry Newenham for their help. One of the staff, standing at the front door, somewhat peremptorily asked, 'Where did you get that Land-Rover?' We told him, and it quickly transpired that he was the diplomat responsible for all British technical support to Ecuador. Until Jan explained, he knew nothing of our proposed assistance to the Ecuadorean Department of Geology and Mines and their collaboration with us.

'We move off as soon as we can, to Riobamba,' Nick added, 'and then Jan and Richard are to go down to Guayaquil to pick up two of our team members who have come out here by sea.'

The embassy official was slowly shaking his head.

'No way will you drive that Rover to Guayaquil,' he said. 'And I can't let you go anywhere without a driver or extra insurance.'

Guayaquil, Ecuador's foremost port, was notorious for muggings, heists and general thievery – a sort of South American Shanghai, old style.

Gloom descended; but after a round of phone calls it was decided that we should buy some more insurance – for £30 – and then just leave. Brian knew we had to go to the dreaded Guayaquil to pick up Mace, Chadwick and the stores, and said that he would square everything after we had gone.

In the busiest hour of the evening, far too late to be setting off on a 126-mile run to Riobamba, Jan took the wheel and with our kit on a roof-rack and five bodies inside we inched our way through the congested city centre with its steep, narrow streets and looming, colonial buildings. After filling the Rover up at a suburban station, and ourselves at a Timballo restaurant, we drove south into open country between the two ridges of the cordillera.

Volcanoes soon appeared on either hand – Atacazo, Antisana, Sinchongua, Corazón, Rumiñahui, Iliniza: some rounded humps, others jagged, snow-covered triangles. In the gathering darkness a most exquisite surprise then loomed up. Near Latacunga a perfect cone, enormous and white, was picked out in the sun's last rays: Cotopaxi, a dormant giant of 19339 feet (5897 metres), climbed by both Alexander Humboldt and Edward Whymper and for a long time believed to be the second highest mountain in the world, lay some ten miles away to the east.

Thought by some to be showing signs of renewed activity, it looked peaceful enough as we drove past it to the earthquake-prone town of Ambato, where we stopped for coffee. About eleven at night we rolled finally into Riobamba, an ancient Inca centre built up by the Spanish in classical gridiron pattern and full of atmosphere. Dark shapes swathed in ponchos stood about in the bus park, each under an identical cardinal's hat. It was not at all like my earlier dream, but equally romantic.

Nick, Adrian and Gerardo were soon lodged in two rooms at the nearby Hotel Metro (reputedly £1 per night and good breakfast), with instructions to rise early, procure a lift of some sort and proceed to the upper Alao valley and our roadhead on the way to Sangay. Meanwhile, without pause, Jan and I would drive on in the Land-Rover, down to the coast to Guayaquil.

About to cross the railway tracks by the station, we saw in the blackness two swinging lights advancing towards us. I got out to investigate and there followed a few moments of pure joy. Two shunters were warning us of the slow approach of a steam locomotive. Lit by street lights, No. 44 of FERROCARRILES ECUATORIANA, in delightful LMS-red livery, came hissing and wheezing along, cow-catcher thrust forward and white smoke billowing from its diamond shaped spark-arrester. Its tender, with 'G & Q' (presumably 'Guayaquil and Quito') in gold, was stacked with the wood that it burned, and it drew behind it three or four cabooses which belonged more to the nineteenth-century Atchison, Topeka and Santa Fé. For me this was an unalloyed return to the excitements of boyhood, and I only regretted it was too dark for photography.

At Cajabamba we left the Pan-American highway and began to climb over the western cordillera. It soon became a nightmare drive, for we were now in darkness and cloud, and the dirt road, unlined, unedged and unfenced, often veered sharply above great chasms. I had taken the wheel just before we had passed, without realizing it, over the col, and as we now dropped down round bend after bend, great lorries, lit like Christmas trees, almost filled the road as they ground interminably upwards. It seemed that I had gone through the tiredness barrier, and as we swung endlessly down into re-entrants and out of them again my eyes, though dead, were out on stalks and quite alert. At a filling station in the steamy foothills I eventually handed over to Jan, who drove on through overhanging banana trees and past rice-fields, where egrets and cranes waded about, elegant and unafraid.

We raced, as fast as spine-jarring pot-holes would permit, over the coastal plains to the thirty-sucre toll bridge over the Daule and Babahoyo rivers into early morning Guayaquil.

We found the Pacific Steam Navigation Company's agents at the corner of Junín and the Malecón Simón Bolívar, which runs along the waterfront.

'The *Orcoma* arrives tonight,' said Alfredo Gaetano, who was to look after us, 'but the port is full, so it will drop anchor way down the Guayas and come in tomorrow perhaps.'

Jan looked glum at the prospect of a day's delay.

'I have to go out to her with the immigration and health people, so you could come in the launch with me and collect your friends tonight.'

We brightened.

'See you at midnight,' he added.

He tried to find us a cheap hotel in which to sleep off our exhaustion, but £6 seemed excessive for just a part of the day, so we drove along the waterfront, past an importunate crowd of car-washers, pimps ('You want my sister? She do jig-a-jig') and self-appointed Land-Rover sentinels.

Guayaquil is the glorious mixture of refinement and squalor often found in South American cities. Overlooking the mud banks of the Guayas and shielded from them by a semicircular colonnade is the grandiose marble statuary depicting Simón Bolívar's famous meeting with José de San Martín in 1822. A hundred yards away men were queuing to use an outshot privy of unspeakable wretchedness where I spent a nervous five minutes shouting 'Ocupado!' as relays of impatient Guayaquileños sought to relieve themselves. In order presumably not to despoil the waters of the Guayas, the loo paper previously bought from an old crone (torn-up municipal *pronunciamentos*, it looked like) had afterwards to be brought out of the dark, evil cabinets in which customers crouched, and dropped into a tin outside each door.

'*Autre pays, autre moeurs*,' I muttered to myself as I went off to buy a couple of bottles of Seven-up.

Inevitably it was at Guayaquil that I underwent the ritual of having something nicked. It happens to everyone who goes there, but it also happens to me everywhere I go. During each expedition I seem fated to fall victim to some light-fingered local. I mollify myself afterwards by saying that it is my little contribution to solving the North–South problem, to giving aid to the Third World by simple redistribution of wealth.

On my first day in Africa in 1966 I folded my jacket and, watched by unseen eyes, hid it under a Land-Rover seat and went into an Addis Ababa bar. It is a tribute to Ethiopia that my love affair with the country survived despite this precipitate lifting of coat, passport, travellers' cheques and wallet. In Jamaica, during six weeks in 1973-4, I had in three separate swoops been relieved of money, wristwatch and camera.

'We must never leave the Land-Rover unattended here even for a minute,' we had agreed.

When I returned with the soft drinks, Jan was lying dozing across the middle seats. The doors were shut and the windows closed tight, but my Olympus 35 mm was gone from the windscreen ledge.

Jan and I then drank a bottle of Chilean wine and lay in the sun watching the flotsam ebbing and flowing in the Guayas. Some young girls came along the levee. They had both cheek and charm, they made a great deal of our blue eyes and it was some solace to be chatted up. Describing their home town one said, '*Hay insectes de todos clases en*

Guayaquil,' and, mindful of the theft of my camera, I could not but agree.

At dusk we drove off to the Rotonda monument, where Bolívar and San Martín stand shaking hands confidently, and turned inland away from them down the long Avenida 9 de Octubre to the Parque Centenario. The port was hard to find, but we soon realized that a new one had been built five miles south of the city.

In this modern installation we had a canteen supper and waited for midnight. We then boarded a launch and set off downriver with Alfredo Gaetano and about twenty others. Nosing round flat, estuarine islands we soon saw the brilliantly illuminated *Orcoma*. We tied up at the foot of the lowered companion-way and were soon laughing and joking in a floating piece of Britain. Ron Mace and Peter Chadwick were roused and within ten minutes they had packed, bid farewell to Captain Turner and been decanted with a stack of kit into the launch.

Back at the port we loaded the Rover and having befriended the *Jefe de Seguridad*, a retired army colonel, over supper, we made short work of customs clearance. Before three a.m. we were rolling again through Guayaquil *en route* for the mountains.

Jan, Ron and I shared the wheel and we all four exchanged news as the heavily laden vehicle was coaxed up the cordillera. When dawn came we marvelled at the precipitous valleys we had skirted in darkness the night before. But somehow they were never quite photogenic enough.

'Fancy a bit of film here?' asked Jan.

'Not really. It's still too much like north Wales,' said Ron.

At Riobamba the steam engine was sadly absent so we passed on directly towards Alao. A rolling country road took us to Licto with its large plaza and solid, stone, Spanish buildings. We dropped to a bridge over the Río Chambo and climbed, with the occasional film-stop, to the last town on our way – Pungalá. We were now in the narrow Alao valley, tending south-westward, and it became a hair-raising, vertiginous drive in whose dangers Jan

Sangay can be seen from tea plantation country to the north-east, but
jungle-clad foothills and big rivers running east towards Brazil make
it an impractical approach route

Quito's modern heart, looking north-east to the Tumbaco valley

Nick Cooke at Alao

Jan Iwandziuk, reconnaissance
leader

The author, back at Sandhurst
after the tragedy

Ron Mace,
photographer, on
board M.V. *Orcoma* at
Liverpool

Cine-cameraman Peter
Chadwick

Adrian Ashby-Smith
in his Zaire River
Expedition shirt

Ecuadorean Indians are descended from the Incas and still speak
Quechua

We passed many of their markets on our way from Quito to the
volcano

seemed to exult, until we emerged into a slender, grassy plain studded with thatched cabins. A patchwork of tilled fields stretched high up the steep sides and into cloud. The greenness was positively Irish, and no doubt the same sort of rainfall prevailed. We were in Alao and at the roadhead.

At the village's only two-storeyed house and the last one on the long, main street we found Nick, Adrian and Gerardo. The British Vulcan Expedition reconnaissance team was met together for the first time.

4

Across the Cordillera

The terrain before us was even worse than we had tra-
versed, and the weather was abominable. . . . Again that
night we had a brief awe-inspiring glimpse of white-hot
ash and lava rising in a fountain from the volcano and
falling back, like fireworks, to splash El Sangay's slopes
with glowing rock.

G. Edward Lewis, 'El Sangay, Fire-breathing Giant of the
Andes', *National Geographic Magazine*, 97, no. 1, January
1950, pp. 117-38

Our three colleagues had had rather a dusty reception in
Riobamba when they had first tried to cadge a Land-Rover
to take them to Alao, but eventually a kindly, cigar-smoking
official in the agricultural service, a young version of Orson
Welles, assigned one to them, with a driver.

At Alao they decanted their kit into the two-storeyed
National Park rest-house, where they were to occupy a
couple of ground-floor rooms. A bed, a table and a few
chairs on the bare earth afforded some comfort. Each of
them tried the bed, but its lumpy mattress made the ground
seem preferable.

The rest-house warden was not in. In fact, he was guiding
Minard Hall, the American geologist, on his ten-day foray
to the Sangay area and was expected back the following
day. So Nick and Gerardo went on their own to the head-
man of Alao, the feudal chief of all the valley, Don Alfonso
Merino.

The Merino family have been entrenched in the valley for
a great many years and have helped most previous expedi-

tions to Sangay, including that of the first modern explorer to reach the volcano's slopes. This was an American, Commander G. M. Dyott, who passed through Alao in 1925, crossed the eastern cordillera, climbed to beyond the snowline and met defeat just 400 feet below the craters.

Old Don Alfonso was at his hacienda. He offered Nick four mules and four guides, and they were to be ready at 6.0 a.m. in two days' time. Adrian then joined Nick and Gerardo to climb to the southern ridge of the narrow, almost Swiss valley. Through fields of wheat and potatoes they toiled up, past tiny, windowless hovels whose thatched roofs were tied down with plaited ropes of straw. Stubby farmers in black or red ponchos and worn grey trilbies stared at them impassively, and children, in their minia-turized adult dress, forgot their flocks of sheep and goats as the strange trio strode past them.

A period of warm-up like this is invaluable to any expedition, but especially so to one which involves climb-ing. Mountain men need to acclimatize not only to the height but to each other. It afforded a chance for Nick to get to know Adrian, Adrian Nick, and both of them Gerardo.

It soon seemed that they were well-matched, and the three formed an easy relationship. Expedition leaders rightly concentrate on choosing a compatible team, and it so far appeared that Jan had done so. Nick found Adrian a quiet, hard-working, if somewhat enigmatic young officer, who did his quartermastering work supremely well. He kept out of everyone's way, always self-effacingly taking the most uncomfortable seat, the heaviest load. He cooked palatable food for us all but ate sparingly himself and, as a vegetarian for whom army tinned rations do not properly cater, never very well. Nick only found it a minor irritation that Adrian's conversation, such as it was, seemed to consist of a string of trendy, often arcane clichés which made him difficult to fathom. What was the man like, Nick wondered, behind this defensive screen?

In his turn, Adrian was immediately on terms with Nick,

who even *looked* to him like a mountaineer, his jaw lined and his eyes crow-footed from squinting up into sunlit snow. Adrian was always ready to respect men of greater rank and experience and never questioned their judgement. He would have followed Nick anywhere.

Gerardo's fractured English made him still a bit of an unknown quantity, but he had a cheerful disposition and seemed willing enough to muck in.

The following morning the advance guard of Haroun Tazieff's French expedition arrived in Alao. They were members of the Ecuadorean army Special Forces, and they wanted to go right over the southern ridge that our friends had climbed the previous day and visit the next valley, the Río Guarguallá valley, where Don Alfonso's son Fausto lived and farmed from an isolated hacienda. This valley might, they had heard, be a better jumping-off point for Sangay. Nick took a lift with them, but the mud road was broken by landslides on the other side of the ridge. They walked down into an almost identical, parallel valley and found Señor Fausto Merino at his door.

He was a splendid, powerful figure, black-bearded, thickly and colourfully clad in leather jerkin, sheepskin chaps, pullover, scarf and woollen cap, and taciturn almost to the point of non-communication.

'This the best place to start,' the Ecuadorean sergeant told Nick after a few moments' halting talk.

Our mules were to have come over from Fausto's valley to his father's, and so Nick stopped them as they were about to set out and announced that the British Vulcan Expedition would make its way to the Guarguallá valley and leave from there on the next day.

When they climbed back into the Alao valley and down to the rest-house Jan, Peter, Ron and I had arrived and our Land-Rover was being unloaded.

'Sooty!' shouted Jan, grinning, as they walked up.

Sooty was Adrian's *alter ego*, a kind of imagined extension of himself which could take some of life's knocks for him and to which he could address his problems.

'Sooty, *OBE*, do you *mind*,' Adrian laughed.

Some of us had not met since the final gathering in an upper room at the Royal Geographical Society, and the atmosphere glowed with bonhomie.

'What have you got for us to eat, Sonny Boy?' Jan asked Adrian.

'The usual filth. Be ready in half an hour.'

Nick told Jan of his decision that we should start from the adjoining valley the next morning and Jan concurred.

As they talked a tall, rangy Ecuadorean wearing a blue construction worker's helmet came down the mud road from the east with a string of pack-laden animals. It was the National Park warden and the packs belonged to Minard Hall who was following an hour or two behind him.

'I don't like it,' said Jan. 'All these Ecuadorean soldiers, and now the American. This place is getting like Snowdonia on an August weekend. I think we ought to get over to Guarguallá tonight.'

'Hey, wait a minute, we've only just arrived,' said Ron. 'Let's get a decent night's sleep in this house.' He had been brusquely woken in his cabin on the *Orcoma* the previous midnight and had driven for much of the day.

'Don't you think we ought to wait for Minard Hall to come in and quiz him about the mountain?' Nick asked.

Minard Hall had once suggested in a letter that he would join up with us and the fact that he had gone off to Sangay earlier and independently had clearly peeved Jan.

'Look, we can't afford to waste any time. This place will be jumping with Frenchmen by tomorrow.'

So just as we finished emptying the Land-Rover we began to load it again. And a curious contest began, in which we strove to get away from the oncoming French, just as Barrie Page and Chris Bonington had chauvinistically manoeuvred to forestall the Italian climbers who had followed them to the foot of the remote Central Tower of Paine in Patagonia in 1962.

With most of our kit on the roof-rack we managed to get

our seven bodies inside the Land-Rover, and at about
5 p.m. Jan drove off. We knew the track over the ridge was
impassable so to reach Fausto's hacienda, just two miles
away as the Ecuadorean crow flies, we had to motor back
to Pungalá and Licto and along a series of perilous, cliff-
hanging roads up to the mouth of the Guarguallá valley.
Dusk fell as we entered it and Jan's temper began to fray as
tiredness sapped his strength.

Nick and Adrian had both been briefly afflicted with
mountain sickness and now it was my turn. My stomach
was all a-churn, and when we once stopped to ask the way
I had to scuttle off into the darkness quickly. It was the
first time in my life I had discharged from both ends
simultaneously.

The track followed the contours into long re-entrants
and seemed endless. So horrifyingly narrow was it that we
were glad of the invisibility of night as Jan, fearing that we
were quite lost, relentlessly urged the Land-Rover round
the sheer rock faces. Each of us had differing and unshake-
able views of our position on the map and nerves were very
edgy when we eventually coasted down into the farm
precincts. The drive had taken over three hours.

I felt so ill that I bedded down in the front of the vehicle
and missed the glass of *aguardiente*, the local fire-water with
which Señor Fausto welcomed us. Jan took the bench
behind me, Nick, Peter, Ron and Gerardo squashed into a
tent, and Adrian, characteristically, slept in the open.

'How do you feel, Richard?' Jan asked huskily.

It was a cloudy dawn and I lay on my back looking up
through the windscreen to the tracery of eucalyptus
branches which loomed over us. The similarities between
Ethiopia and Ecuador came to mind once again. How odd
it was, I was now thinking, that the eucalyptus which
flourishes in both countries should have been introduced
into them from Australia at roughly the same time.

The previous night I had swallowed several Lomotil

tablets and I now concentrated my mind on my stomach, which seemed fragile but at ease.

'Fine,' I said, 'and you?'

'Pretty rotten,' Jan replied, his pallid face nestled in an army sleeping-bag.

'Come on, you peasants,' said Adrian, shoving two mugs of coffee through the open window.

'Did you know, Adrian, that the eucalyptus . . .'

Drowsily I told him the story because it was the sort of useless gem of information that he loved to jot down later in his notebooks.

That morning the mules were slowly assembled, and while the guides were loading our rucksacks onto them Peter and Ron began their first sustained spell of film-making. As the Bolex whirred Nick several times unzipped the tent-flap, stuck his head out and sniffed the morning air in convincing fashion. Similarly Señora Merino was asked to emerge from her hacienda and scatter grain before some turkeys. So bedazzled was she at the prospect of stardom that she went to change into her smartest blue poncho, and then further maddened the film team by dashing inside before each take to apply yet more mascara. The resultant shots are unusable: she looks not at all the rugged frontiers-woman at the last outpost of civilization, but more like something out of *Harper's Bazaar*.

Nick Cooke was chafing to get started when Adrian appeared, looking distinctly grey.

'You OK, Adrian?'

'Just lost my breakfast.'

We were all gradually succumbing to what we called Atahualpa's Revenge.

Eventually the filming was finished, the tent was struck and the Land-Rover was loaded with all those items that between the mules and ourselves we couldn't carry and we felt we could just about do without. We bade farewell to the Merinos, locked the vehicle and formed into a column.

The impassive Callisto was our chief guide, a proud figure

in his poncho and leather chaps. Riding with him was a round-faced boy with twinkling brown eyes, whose name we never learned, then Anacleto, as inscrutable as most of his race, and Ramón, whose permanent expression seemed to hover somewhere between dark suspicion and incredulity. Grey trilbies on their heads (except for Ramón, who sported a Panama), their feet thrust into wooden, box stirrups, they pirouetted about, organizing the four pack mules.

It was now that we noted one marked change from the high days of nineteenth-century exploration: whereas early pioneers rode in some state while their *portadores* trotted behind them carrying folding camp beds, tents, medical chests and other paraphernalia, it was made quite clear that our four guides were to ride while we legged it alongside them. When it was obvious that Jan was too ill to walk, it was with the greatest difficulty that we got one of the guides to surrender his mount to him. Nevertheless, for a modest fifty sucres per day (just over £1 at the late 1976 rate) they put up with much hardship, and we did not begrudge them their sturdy little mules.

Not until 11 a.m. did we finally move out. It was as much our acclimatization problems – only Peter Chadwick and Nick seemed unaffected – as the interminably slow film-work that caused the delays which irritated Nick so much. He realized that three days' march across fifteen difficult miles lay ahead of us and that we probably wouldn't reach our first objective before darkness.

The early stages lay along sunken lanes reminiscent of Devon, past farmsteads and grazing land. We were still in Merino territory. We then dropped to cross the Guarguallá and cut up the valley of a tributary, the Cholumpallá. Here the column moved up over exposed shoulders of tough grasses and began a protracted traverse along a contour line high above the tributary. Sunny morning turned to cloudy, chilly afternoon. Jan sat slumped in his saddle like a sack of King Edwards.

'Are you managing, old boy?' I asked.

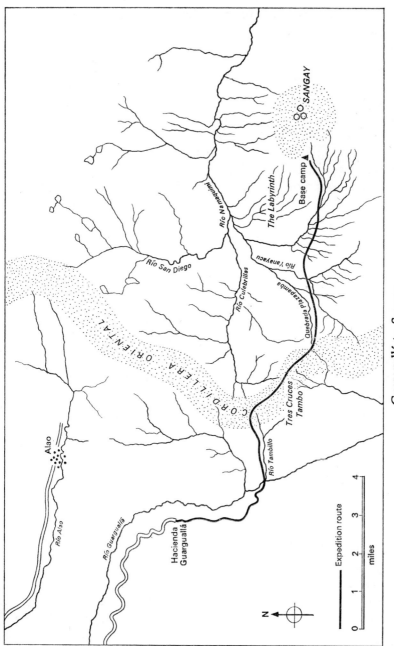

Guarguallá to Sangay

'It's not the best place to have constant diarrhoea,' he replied bitterly.

We were now in the *páramo* grasslands which were to prevail all the way to the volcano. The hillsides and the boggy plains were alike covered in great tussocks. To leap from one to another would have been ankle-breaking folly; the only answer was to follow the mules and slop along the muddy runnels between them.

At 3 p.m. we stopped to open a few tins of meat and oatmeal biscuits. Pushing on, the column became extended over about a mile of open ground. We were all wet through and now plunged into beds of sphagnum without bothering to make a detour. I was near the rear and felt that I wasn't going too well, even for Day One. But Nick and Adrian seemed in very good order and Peter, despite something of a beer gut and the unhealthy life-style we automatically associate with photographers of London model girls, was striding along in cracking form.

Dusk fell as we reached the tributary's source. We might have camped there at the head of the valley but the guides, who had been chivvying us along with cries of '*Más rápido!*', wanted to press on. We toiled up a steep grass spur towards the watershed of the eastern cordillera, and just over a shoulder Nick found that they had stopped and off-loaded the mules. He was most disgruntled – there was no water anywhere near. But it was a *fait accompli*. Adrian began to sort out the heaps of kit, damp now in the descending mist. 'Welcome to the Andes, home of the bean,' he said to me as I dropped wearily to the ground. We were on a fairly flat platform, but no tent could be put up among such closely massed tussocks. So we each found our own place to lie up and the night resounded to the snap and crinkle of polythene as we bedded down in our survival bags. 'Little Miss Muffet sat on a tuffet . . .' I intoned to myself as I wedged in between three or four of them. Nearby the ghostly white shape of a mule cropped the grass, and as I drifted into sleep I wondered how well he was tethered, if at all.

It was a grisly awakening when, just after 5 a.m., we pulled on socks, trousers and boots – all covered in hoar frost. We had crashed out supperless and were to move off breakfastless: 'Brunch later' was the promise. But it didn't convince the guides, who refused to go on further with us. This is a fairly stock situation on expeditions, and it required a flash of slav temperament from Jan to sting them into cooperation. They would go on, they said, until ten or eleven o'clock.

We climbed to the actual watershed – Loma de Chesclós – at nearly 12000 feet and negotiated an awkward traverse on a steep scarp where a landslide had torn away the normal trail. As dawn broke we looked down upon mile after mile of silent, open grassland and not a single tree. Below us were some of the headstreams of the Amazonian river system. Swallows dipped about us and light brown hawks with white-barred wings soared above.

Following Callisto's arm I saw a thatched hut about two miles away to the south-east.

'Tambo Tres Cruces,' he said.

A *tambo* is a rest-house and there are two or three dotted about in the wilderness which leads to Sangay; they are used by occasional hunting parties and have a corral for their animals in front.

It was good to have confirmation of a name on one of the earlier expedition maps we had, and the knowledge that we were moving forward on more or less the right line.

The first modern approach to Sangay, by Commander Dyott in 1925, had been by a more northerly route – up the Alao valley, over the cordillera and down the Río Culebrillas (Little Snakes River). Four years later Robert T. Moore followed the same track. It took him fifteen days to get from his camp in the Culebrillas valley to the base of the cone. But after two unsuccessful attempts he was the first to scale Sangay: 'dense clouds of light-coloured gas poured from the orifice', but otherwise the volcano slumbered.

Following in what was so far a wholly American tradition, G. Edward Lewis and Wallace Estill traced the same route to the Río Culebrillas in 1946. But this was just a training run for them, as Lewis had spotted a better approach from the air three years before. So they soon returned to the valley of the Guarguallá River, whence they pioneered our route – to its source, over the cordillera to the Tres Cruces Tambo, where they had to leave their horses and proceed on foot along a line of knife-edged ridges to Sangay. It was Lewis's map that I had in my rucksack. Clearly our guides had taken us on a similar but slightly northerly line.

Lewis and Estill had circled to the south of Sangay and climbed it to 16000 feet, but it was too active for them to want to go further.

Sebastian Snow and Chris Bonington, sent out by the *Daily Telegraph Magazine* in 1966 to get pictures of an inaccessible and highly volatile volcano, chose Sangay. With Jorge Larrea they climbed it first from the south, via Macas, but Bonington was not satisfied with his pictures and so they approached it again – this time from the Alao valley and the Río Culebrillas (or so I judge from Bonington's map*). They climbed it again, but the crater was unphotogenically filled with dense steam and mist swirled all around:

I spent an hour on the brink of that crater, hoping for a clearance – even half-hoping for an eruption – to get some truly spectacular photographs, yet at the same time fearful of my own prospects of survival in such an event.

It was back at the camp that an Indian ran in with news of the death by drowning of Chris's firstborn son, Conrad, in the lowlands of Scotland. Sangay had let Chris off lightly, but fate had meanwhile been cruel to his wife, Wendy.

Spread out now like long-distance runners we plodded along through the *páramo*. In the lead, our guides on their

---

* *The Next Horizon*, Chris Bonington (Gollancz, 1973).

mules often disappeared from view. The landscape stretched in front of us like rumpled bedclothes, and we were soon following a contour line round a succession of pyramidal hills, to emerge onto a bare saddle overlooking a broad, green valley. Here the mules came to a stop and were relieved of their loads. This is where they were to leave us and return to Guargualla and Shanks's pony was to take over.

'Gerardo, these mules must come out here again in five days' time and meet us,' said Jan. 'Can you tie that up with the guides?'

'That'll be August 14th, will it?' asked Gerardo.

'Yes, and I want it down in writing,' Jan added darkly. 'This morning they gave us the "White-man-speak-with-forked-tongue" bit, and so I want no misunderstanding about the return rendezvous.'

Gerardo settled amid the tussocks with Callisto and the boy and a letter was drawn up, which asked Señor Merino to release them in time for the required date.

Painfully, then, we redistributed the burdens we were now to carry ourselves – camp stores, climbing gear, heavy army 'compo' rations – and helped each other to hoist them to our backs.

With a cheerful '*Hasta luego!*' Callisto and the boy rode off with the two pack-mules in train, and we were left with Anacleto and Ramón, who looked more glum and sour than ever as he eyed the rucksack we had given him, which was now filled solidly to the drawstrings with tins of food.

We then slithered for 600 feet down a steep zig-zag of mud, reached the plain and marched across it to where a lone, thatched hut stood within its corral: Plaza Pamba. Fleetingly the sun appeared, so we dried our clothes, brunched on hot curried chicken and tea and repacked our rucksacks.

Amid the chaos of our scattered gear Ramón stood pathetically, his spaniel eyes cast sadly down.

'*Calcetines*,' he said to no one in particular, and splayed out his hands in a universal Third World gesture.

Between his half-mast trousers and a pair of thin, laceless shoes were bare ankles and feet. We fished out a spare pair of socks for him.

Leaving behind a cache of tinned food for our return journey, we set off about 2 p.m. to follow a river into a steep-sided valley. Anacleto said it was the Little Snakes River, but it could hardly be the Río Culebrillas of Lewis's map. All rivers with winding courses are perhaps apt to be likened to little snakes.

The going became extremely wet, and we slopped along through marshes on either bank and frequently through the river itself. Heavy rain now fell and so the damp became all-pervasive: despite our anoraks only a small area around the crotch and stomach seemed to stay dry.

At one point we crossed a river by a slender log that had been washed downstream. Ron looked at it apprehensively.

'Who do you think I am, Olga Korbut?'

He had done prodigies in getting his weight down for the expedition, but the chances of his beamwork ever putting him in the same league as the svelte little Russian were nil.

At 3.45 p.m. we reached the junction with the Río Yanayacu and shortly afterwards left the river system to climb sharply up a grass arête and onto a ridge. For three hours we were to pick our steps carefully through shrubs and tussocks, with precipitous slopes and often landslides on either hand. Our route lay along a crest which undulated eerily through the wet mists like a big dipper.

To burden our porters to the full we had given Ron Mace's massive green rucksack, a spanking new one on a tubular framework, to Anacleto, who strode along with Nick Cooke at the head of the column. Ramón, with his equally taxing load, was told off to be whipper-in, but he found it tedious to wait about and constantly forged on to the front. This meant that the back markers, uncertain as dusk fell whether they were still on the right ridge, stumbled onwards from summit to summit shouting to each other hopefully through the enveloping murk.

By nightfall we had once again not reached our planned objective. But we found a small triangular platform on a hilltop, Anacleto and Ramón cut grass to clear the area and provide bedding, and this time we did pitch the tents. Once more, despite the heavy drizzle, we hadn't sufficient water for cooking, so supper was another attenuated affair of cold corned beef and tinned cake.

We lay damp and stiff in our cramped corners, and if any of us had forgotten what it was we were all to pit ourselves against, a salutary reminder came about 9 p.m. In the distance, but quite loud, was a sudden crack and rumble. Sangay, described by Dr Teodoro Wolf as early as 1892 as one of the most active volcanoes in the world, was blowing off.

Peter, Ron and Adrian had a wretched night of it because Nick, to save on weight, had foolishly decided not to take their flysheet, and the flimsy tent itself leaked horribly. But Jan decreed that, at whatever cost in time, we must have a porridge breakfast, and so spirits were quite soon restored.

By 9 a.m. we were moving off again along the seemingly endless chain of ridges. Surely Sangay must now be near? We were on our last day's march, after all. Despite our collective experience there were some of us still naïve enough to ask the porters those timeless questions: 'How much further to go?', 'Where is it?' and 'How long will it take to get there?' And they got the same timeless responses – an impatient wave of the hand and a shrug of the shoulders. In Crete the mountain farmers measure distances in cigarettes. In Ecuador no unit of measurement seemed to have any meaning for our porters.

'Don't worry them,' said Jan. 'It's the mushroom syndrome.'

'What do you mean?' asked Peter.

'They keep you in the dark, feed you a load of shit and tell you you'll come out all right in the end.'

The truth probably is that the porters only rarely penetrated these regions on their occasional deer-hunting forays, they judge distances in broad terms of days' journeys and have no name for the minor geographical features.

After two hours we dropped steeply down an L-shaped ridge and reached a river. Crossing it, we battled straight up through the tussocks on the other side. This happened twice more. The long ridge-walk was over and we were now moving across the grain of the country.

About mid-day, lying fourth or fifth in the column, I had just hauled up onto a crest and saw the bright blobs of the orange and red anoraks of the leaders as they dropped down ahead of me into the valley. I sank back exhausted to rest on my pack for a couple of minutes. I was too sodden to think of getting my pipe and tobacco out so I simply stared up into white mist. As I did so the clouds seemed suddenly to part like a theatre curtain, and where I expected there to be sky I saw revealed a massive volcano thrusting up into the blue – still, silent, perfect in its symmetry.

In the valley bottom were huge, flat-topped bergs of plum-coloured lava ash which had at some distant time flowed, glacier-like, from the mountain. They were some forty feet high and looked pretty solidly compacted. A northward-running river had cut into them, creating vertical-sided islands of lava. Beyond were grass-covered ridges, presumably also of lava, then a midriff of sepia rocks and ash and finally a magnificent cone of snow. Billows of white smoke trailed lazily from the summit.

I lay in the wet grass and marvelled at so much raw nature, so anticipated and yet so surprising, until a veil of cloud was again drawn across the whole prospect.

5
Going Up

Farther on, at a point where we come out of the forest, all at once – as if someone had thrown a burning coal on the black velvet – there is red light, a glowing stove hung in the sky; and silhouetted against it is the outline of the volcano Sangay.

Ludwig Bemelmans, *The Donkey Inside*

With infinite weariness I toiled up the gentle lava slope towards one of our orange tents. From far down in the valley I had heard the clink of metal poles as Nick, Adrian and Peter had struggled in the cold rain to pitch our base camp on a flat platform at about 12375 feet. Now I had made it, but I was too ill-acclimatized and drained of energy to do more than stand for a few moments and watch them adjusting the guy ropes. Where the pegs would not hold in the loose ash Nick and Adrian anchored them with the surprisingly light, pyroclastic rocks which lay scattered around.

'Any sign of Ron and Gerardo?' Nick asked me.

'Ron was behind me,' I said, 'but he was making very heavy weather of coming down that last hill.'

After my private view of Sangay I had found it difficult enough myself, but had reached the river and the first lava flow. The route then crossed and recrossed what was at that moment a broad, shallow stream, and then twisted up a couloir of ash onto the smooth top of the berg. Here rocks the size of grapefruit lay stuck in the dusty surface like caraway seeds in a brown bun.

c

SANGAY SURVIVED

'I'll go and see if I can find them,' said Adrian and strode off down.

Peter Chadwick had been standing holding the ridge-pole. Now his lower jaw juddered visibly, and he thrust his hands hopefully under his armpits for warmth.

'One of the . . . great things about climbing in the . . . Andes,' he stammered, 'is that you can be bloody wet and cold one minute . . . and bloody wet and cold the next.'

The porters had no tent, but were away cutting grass for an improvised double bed. Jan and Nick built them a low wall of rocks over which a groundsheet could be slung.

'What a hellish spot to come to for one's summer hols,' I mused, as Jan and I put our tent up. 'I think I'd rather be in Benidorm or Bognor Regis.'

This was not a serious observation: even in the worst extremities of an expedition the alternative prospect of a traditional package holiday holds little appeal for me.

Adrian, with apparently boundless energy, was returning up the hill with Ron's unwieldy pack on his back. When Ron had given Anacleto his brand-new Berghaus he was given in exchange a large plastic bag carried by a single, biting rope across the chest.

'Positively Dantesque place, isn't it?' I observed. 'Sooty must feel at home.'

'None of your infernal cheek,' he said, hoisting the rope over his tousled head with its grubby sweatband.

To have reached Sangay ahead of the French induced in us a great wave of chauvinistic exultation. Beating Haroun Tazieff's party was, we felt, some sort of triumph.

Adrian turned and shouted, 'Cop that, you Frogs!' in the general direction of the empty valley.

'Iwandziuk rules, OK?' I bellowed after him.

We could not know how wholly we would later be dependent on the French and how desperately grateful for their kindnesses.

Jan and Nick were already in conference. We were to be in the Sangay area for three days. What were our plans?

'I think we should spend the first one route finding,' said Nick. 'Get maybe halfway up.'

'Yes. Then we'll make the ascent proper the next day, and collect a few rock samples on the last and maybe look at some alternative routes.'

'We'll have to make an alpine start in the morning,' added Nick. 'About four-thirty or five or so.'

'Do you really think so?' asked Jan. 'I think we deserve just one leisurely morning. After all, we've had a couple of bastards so far, and we're only going up two or three thousand feet.'

'I don't know,' said Nick, but general opinion was in favour of a more relaxed reveille.

'Look at Ron,' Jan added, as if to reinforce the point.

Ron and Gerardo were struggling painfully up the hill.

'We get lost,' shouted Gerardo.

Ron looked puffed and blown as his leaden feet dragged.

'It's these boots,' he said, but it was clearly also the speed with which he'd reached this altitude. Peter lent him a pair of dry trousers, and they both crawled into the tent to change and rest and check their photographic gear for damp.

Peter had 5000 feet of Eastman colour negative 16 mm in three plastic bags one within the other. But the bags had ripped and he was apprehensively opening up a few tins.

'Quick, Pete . . . Sangay! You can see it!' shouted Jan, and Peter spilled from his tent to assemble his tripod and Bolex before the late afternoon sun sank and the volcano was again obscured.

Adrian had been all this time outside rummaging for food tins and soon Jan began to prepare some supper. No orders were being given; we were all instinctively fulfilling our roles, which made Jan's responsibilities that much easier. Ron, for instance, was taking still shots of Sangay with his Nikon, while Nick was writing up his diary and, in the manner of all correctly trained officers, preparing his plans for the following day.

Later, he said to Ron, 'I'd like you to stay and look after the base camp tomorrow. We'll only be doing a bit of preliminary route finding, and I think you should acclimatize as much as possible before the ascent itself.'

Ron, whose feet were now giving him much pain, was happy to acquiesce – especially as he knew that all being well he would make it on the Thursday.

'I've saved for a year to come on this trip – and given up my job,' he added, 'so I'm not going to let the bugger elude me.'

This was the first time for three nights that we had camped near water. On arrival we had celebrated with mugs of sweet, milkless tea and now I watched Jan as he made some porridge.

'That's a good, thick constituency,' he said.

'You mean solid, like Ebbw Vale or Cheltenham?'

'Pass your mess-tins up,' he said, and we ate it lying in our sleeping bags in the warmth of the tents.

This warmth was short-lived for Nick, Ron, Peter and Gerardo, who passed a disastrous night. It rained and it rained and their tent, minus flysheet, quickly became sodden. Our system was to keep one set of dry clothes for sleeping in and another set, permanently muddy and wet, for walking and climbing in. Now the two sets were almost indistinguishable, though Nick and the others nevertheless went through the motions of changing them in the morning.

'W-When we get back home,' said Peter, 'w-we'll be so used to putting on wet socks and trousers that we'll go and rinse them in the b-basin first.'

Fortunately, it was a day of patchy sunshine, and Ron was able to get the sleeping bags partially dried, and to repack the film stock in its plastic bags.

'H-How much . . .' stammered Peter.

'"How much is that llama in the window?"' Adrian carolled.

'. . . f-film . . . do you reckon . . . we should take, Ron?'

Peter distributed two or three rolls in plastic bags for each person to carry up and at about 10 a.m. six of us set off, accompanied by Anacleto.

Immediately there was a delicate problem. We had to climb off the ash-berg on which we were camped and into a deep ravine. This involved a near-vertical descent of some fifty feet on very loose material. A shower of dislodged stones nearly broke Peter's camera lens as he filmed it.

At first, the valley sides were thickly covered in tufts of grass and tiny flowers. We sweated up a long 20-degree slope in the warm sun, peeling off superfluous anoraks, cagouls and pullovers. Here and there we found boot-marks, which could have been made by Minard Hall a few days before.

After an hour or so we emerged into a chaos of bare, unvegetated lava ridges. At a large boulder Nick decided to turn right, and he tapped an orange marker flag in the ground to aid our return.

The going, in places, was fiendishly difficult. The ridges were made up of small particles of lava ash which reacted like ball-bearings as we tried to get a foothold in them. I became like Robert the Bruce's spider as I slowly fought my way up to the crest. Once over the shoulder the incessant rain had compacted the ash into a slippery but firm skin, pockmarked here and there by the boulder bombs of earlier eruptions.

A brown hawk circled above the chill, dead landscape. And there were indications of other sorts of wild life: Jan found some curious pug marks which could not possibly be those of deer, the only large animals so far recorded in the Sangay area. Anacleto said, '*Danta! Danta!*' But could tapir occur at as high an altitude as this?

Nick and Anacleto led at a measured pace, Jan and Adrian followed. Peter showed amazing stamina as he skittered about over the lava, filming the slow-moving column from various angles. Gerardo and I brought up the rear, chatting desultorily in Spanglish. He paused occasionally to take a swing at a boulder with his geological hammer, while I toiled up with an ice-axe, planting my weary legs in the boot-marks which zig-zagged ahead of me up the banks of lava, and pausing for breath about every ten seconds.

The green-clad ridges of our camp area were dropping away now into the swirling mist. The only sound was of the distant river curling clockwise around the western and northern flanks of the volcano. We called it variously the Río Volcán or the Río Sangay but it was actually a headstream of the Río Namaquimi. (There *are* two rivers, the Volcán and the Sangay, but they flow off the southern and eastern flanks.)

As we reached the snowline it began to rain and anoraks and cagouls reappeared. While Peter changed the spool in his camera Jan stooped to build a small cairn of rocks and Adrian wrote 'sooty' in the snow. Our choice of route lay between the snow-filled couloirs and the exposed ribs of rocks which ran in neat lines down the mountain like

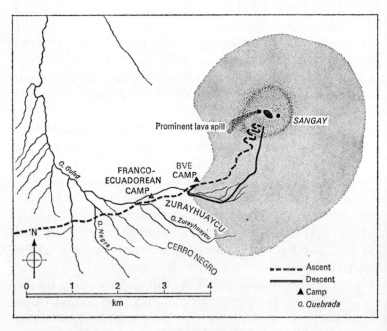

The approaches to Sangay (Based on the 1:50 000 Carta Croquis Planimtérico, ÑV-B1 201, Lago Tinguichaca, of the Instituto Geográfico Militar in Quito, November 1973)

collapsed dry stone walls. The snow was soft and exhausting to plough through, so we hacked up the heaps of rock
which was difficult enough.

The rain turned to snow, ice formed on our rucksacks
and a blizzard swept over the exposed ribs of Sangay with
some force. Peter's beard was spectacularly encrusted when
he again crouched under a boulder to reload his Bolex.

'Let's just get up to that shoulder over there,' shouted
Nick.

We were attacking from the west, but if the wind remained southerly we hoped tomorrow to traverse over to a
southern ridge so that the sulphurous gases from Sangay's
fumaroles would be blown away from us.

'Maybe if this storm lifts we'll see a good route.'

We plodded up at funereal pace but at the shoulder the
snow swirled even more thickly and visibility was diminish-
ing. We were at 14025 feet and above us we could still just
see a smooth, broad snow-field which looked manageable.

It was 2.10 p.m. and Nick decided we should turn back.
Peter, for one, was glad because there was condensation in
his camera and the viewfinder had clouded over.

The return was easy and exhilarating: we ran down the
snow couloirs, digging heels firmly in; we slid over the
greasy shoulders of lava, checking off our flags one by one.
We were back at camp in three-quarters of an hour.

It had all been pretty straightforward so far. The volcano
had been quiet – we had heard nothing since that distant
crack and rumble on the second night of our march in. As
we relaxed in the late afternoon sun and took more pictures,
coils of disgorged smoke, sometimes black, sometimes
white, drifted silently northwards from the summit. From
the mountaineering point of view tomorrow seemed easy
and we settled with light hearts to our curried chicken,
stew, potatoes and fruit salad.

After the tragedy that was to come we often wondered
whether the presence of a volcanologist, rather than simply
a geologist, would have made any difference. Could Peter
Francis have discerned signs which might have led him to

make us wait another day or two or to move round to another angle of approach?

To our inexperienced eyes all seemed set as fair as it could be. Ron was looking perkier and was raring to tackle the climb. The weather was good when Nick woke at 4 a.m. It was half an hour before the rest of us stirred in our bags, but porridge, again, proved an excellent revivifier.

'Come on, everyone,' Nick said. 'We must crack on. Remember we have another three and a half thousand feet to do above where we got to yesterday.'

Gerardo was still dozing and indicated that he did not feel well enough to climb that day and would remain at base. It was 6.30 a.m. before the six of us – Anacleto also stayed down with Ramón – dropped into the ravine beyond the camp. This was half an hour later than Nick had planned.

If anything could be said to be fortunate about Thursday, 12 August, it was these two circumstances: if Gerardo had not ducked out of the climb he might have perished, and certainly could not have played such a key role in the rescue; if we had left on time we would have been half an hour further up the mountain when the holocaust overwhelmed us.

I had gone several minutes ahead of the others. The previous day I had realized I was the slowest ship in the convoy and so now wanted to establish an early lead. As I left the grassy ridges behind, Nick, Adrian and Peter, then Jan and Ron, caught me up. We were all soon at our turning point of the day before.

Every now and then the sun came through, but even when it was obscured the glare from the whiteness around us was damaging. Our snow goggles were invaluable. Commander Dyott, in 1925, had had to turn back when the sun came out at 16800 feet. He had no goggles and was blinded for several days.

Nick took a route straight up the big snow-field. There were some sharp ascents which made the heart race, but we settled down to traversing back and forth across its face.

The snow was firm and we were easily able to kick steps in its patina of ice. Good balance was enough, and we climbed unroped, with an occasional steadying swing from the ice-axe. The angle of repose of volcanic ash and rock is between 30 and 35 degrees, so it was somewhat like zig-zagging across the roof of a house.

All that day we never saw the top of Sangay but soon we were shrouded in a particularly thick mist. Endlessly we laboured to and fro, legs working mechanically, mind in neutral.

Once my thoughts drifted back to the cavernous bar in the hotel we had stayed at in Miami. As an escape from the present desolation I recalled how four of us had sat at a table being served gin and tonics by sparsely clad bar girls. Better than that, there had been a fashion show laid on by Oui Lingerie and Jewelry. A well-designed little blonde called Diane had come to our table and chatted us up, first of all in an evening gown, then in a bikini and finally in a baby-doll shift. Glazed by gin, it was a moment or two before I had realized that the shift was so constructed to reveal what was normally covered, and vice versa. Expeditions are all contrasts, I thought, and life is the better for it.

Some way up the snow-field I got into a good rhythm and began to go really well. I drew away from Jan, who seemed to be flagging, and Ron, just ahead of him, who was having a lot of trouble kicking into the ice and kept falling, especially at the hair-pin bends. Above, the three front runners often disappeared into the mist, but we all had to stop for frequent intakes of the thin air and so from time to time I would concertina almost up to them.

It was while I was once paused in this way that I sensed a new menace: clouds of sulphurous gases suddenly swirled around us. The only recourse was to close the eyes and mouth, suspend breathing and wait. By and by, it seemed to disperse. Peter said afterwards that he had been disturbed by a BBC World Service news item he had heard on the *Orcoma* about a party of Japanese children who had been suffocated by sulphur fumes on a volcano when the wind had suddenly changed direction. If this happened on Sangay he planned to fling himself off and slide down the ice. Having fallen already a few times he judged that it was possible to start and stop at will on the kind of slope we were on.

The climb seemed interminable. Surely the snow would soon give way to hot volcanic ashes as we neared the

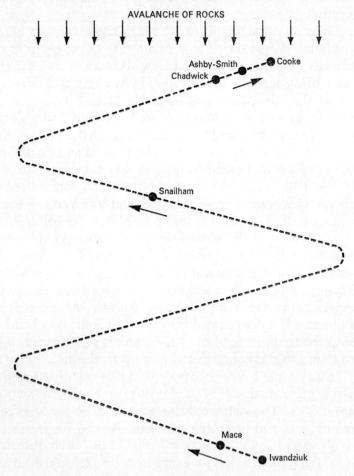

Position of team on snow-field at time of eruption, 12.30 p.m.
12 August 1976

crater? Descriptions of this phenomenon by both Bonington and Snow were fresh in my mind.

Nick stopped once to let the rest of us catch up. He seemed worried by our lack of progress. It was already noon and the sheet of white stretched inexorably upwards. Jan's decision was for Nick, Adrian and Peter to push on at their own natural pace and the rest to follow at theirs and perhaps have not quite so long at the crater.

So on we moved, Nick kicking steps for us all. The absence of points of reference – not a boulder or bump to break up the unrelieved whiteness – had a mesmerizing effect. If it had not been for gravity and my sense of balance I might have been on the flat or on a sheer wall, I sometimes felt.

What next happened has become deeply etched on my memory.

Our reconnaissance of Sangay was aborted with terrifying suddenness. No tremor of the earth, no warning cough or rumble, but a deafening crack and roar somewhere just above and slightly to the left of us. For perhaps five or six seconds the sky reverberated and a thunderous din prevailed, comparable perhaps to an artillery barrage in World War One.

Then it died away. The air stilled for a second or two and I glanced quickly up into the mist. An avalanche of black rocks and boulders, some as big as dustbins, some smaller, was plummeting out of it and rocketing down the icy slopes towards us, through us and over us.

6

Blast-off

Each explosion shoots out glowing fragments of semi-solid lava high into the air. . . . When they hit the ground, they may stop abruptly, embedding themselves still glowing, fuming and sizzling slightly in the loose ash; or they may bounce off, to leap down the steep sides of the cone in a series of great bounds, developing a rapid spin as they do so, and whirring downhill like cannon balls. . . .

Peter Francis, *Volcanoes*

Nick had just checked the altimeter which he carried slung round his neck. We were nearly at 16000 feet (over 4800 metres), and it was about 12.30 p.m.

Each of us who survived has his individual impression of these few seconds. Nick wrote:

The air . . . was black with debris. Ash, gravel and burning stones as big as soup plates or larger. I fell to a crouch and covered my head with my arms. A terrific rain of stones hit me, particularly on the head. I started falling down the snow-slope, fighting to slow down and control my descent. Just as I thought my speed was under control came another smashing blow on the back of the head. I thought that I was finished, either from the blow or the fall. Instinctively I kept . . . digging in hands and feet.

Jan's memory is vivid but limited in range. Searching his mind for clues he has subsequently recalled a loud noise 'like rolling drums'. This might be the eruption, or any traumatic experience inside his head between the eruption and the moment he regained full consciousness in hospital. Later medical evidence suggested that he hooked his right arm over his head to protect it, but he cannot recall dropping to the ground.

Peter Chadwick's account runs:

A terrifying, deep roar that seemed to come from all around us. I can remember thinking very clearly, 'Is this an actual eruption and shall I throw myself down the ice, or am I going to look a fool if I do and nothing happens?' I threw myself down the slope. As I gathered speed I looked back to see what was happening. It was Armageddon – the sky up above was filled with rocks spewing out of the volcano and then landing and rolling down the slope straight towards us. I put my hands over my head and tried to slide faster, hoping that I would be going nearly as fast as the rocks when they caught up with me. I waited, hearing a great rumbling noise behind as I sped on. When the rocks did reach me most of them were going not much faster than I was, and it felt as though I had been sitting on a wall which had collapsed and the rubble and I were going down together. But other rocks, some of them two feet across, were going much faster than I was and would go whistling past and bounce on down the slope at a terrific speed. The number of these began to decrease and I felt more worried now about the pace I was going at, hurtling down the mountain perhaps to go flying over a cliff at the bottom. I dug my heels in to try to slow down – with little effect. Then, wallop! I was hit by one of the last flying rocks. There was a searing pain in my right arm, far worse than anything I had ever felt before, and the arm went flapping round and round uncontrollably in front of me. My first reaction was that the arm had come off completely. I nearly lost consciousness . . . and I think several small stones hit me on the head. Semi-conscious, I thought, 'I *must* stop!' I seemed to be going faster and faster all the time. If I could just slow down I might live. I turned over on my stomach and spread-eagled, pressing my left, unbroken, arm and legs down as hard as I could. My right arm bounced about but strangely did not really hurt any more. Gradually I began to slow down and I turned back again to resume the sitting position, where I felt more in control and could see what was coming at the end of the ice-field.

Then Richard appeared at one side, clutching *his* right arm. I can remember as we slid down, both stunned, having a sur-realistically normal conversation.

I said, 'I seem to have broken my arm.'

'So have I, blast it!'

'Bloody nuisance, isn't it?'

'Yes. I suppose we'll have to drop out of the expedition.'

All this time Peter had had his rucksack on his back with the Bolex cine-camera inside it. Two of its lenses were smashed but otherwise it was perfectly serviceable afterwards. But Peter was to shoot no more film, as it could not easily be operated with the left arm alone, and he was anyway left with only an ultra-telescopic lens.

Like Nick I had instinctively crouched down and covered my head with an arm. Small stones and gravel winged me and one grapefruit-sized rock thudded into the small of my back, but I remained poised on my stance in the snow for several seconds. Then one biggish chunk – I have a fleeting image of it being about the dimensions of a rugger ball – smashed into my right arm just above the elbow, which was probably protruding slightly over the line of my body. The arm, like Peter's, was flung round and my hand fluttered momentarily in front of my face. I felt very little pain and my dominant emotion was one of relief that the arm was still attached. The impetus of the blow knocked me off my foothold, however, and I slid down through the mist, slithering, spinning and scrabbling on the ice-encrusted snow. After a while I seemed to relax, and had little fear of where my momentum might take me. By and by, I dug my heels in and stopped. As I did so a grey, pyroclastic rock, as big as an army boot, rolled slowly past me and came to rest in the snow. Hissing quietly, it settled slowly into its ice matrix.

Nick had slid down with the rest of us and on the way had been struck a savage blow on the back of his leg, above the knee. Rocks had cannoned off his head, too, and as he came to a stop rivulets of blood coursed down into his eyes and filled his snow goggles. He was high above Peter and me, and lay on his stomach imagining us all to be still above him. He then decided what was surely in all our minds – that the reconnaissance would have to be abandoned – and several times blew three shrill blasts on his whistle. There was no answer from the upper slopes, the volcano was tranquil again and as he turned around the sun seemed to be dissipating the mist. Far below he saw Ron in his navy blue anorak and the synthetic, brown, gaucho-style over-trousers he had borrowed from Gerardo, and further down more scattered specks of orange and red. He sat up and began to glissade down towards them.

He came first to Ron, who was sitting up, his face puffed, his left ear filling with blood and his breathing stertorous. Nick decided to bring him down to join the rest of the team, caught hold of a leg and continued to slide down the snow.

In the thin sunlight we slowly gathered ourselves together again. All six of us had been tumbled some 2000 feet down the ice-field and were now at about the point we had climbed to the day before (14250 feet).

Peter stood up unsteadily. One window of his spectacles had been knocked out, and as he was so short-sighted all was a blur. But he realized he was one of the few of us still with working legs and called out, 'Shall I go down and get some help?'

'Yes,' I said, standing up, 'and I reckon I'd better come with you.'

I stumbled towards him, holding my right wrist with my left hand. But, looking down, I noticed a trail of blood on the snow and saw that it was dripping from my sleeve.

'You go on,' I said to Peter. 'I'll follow you.' And I waited for Nick to come down to us.

The other three lay crumpled in the snow like broken rag dolls. It was a pitiful sight. Ron sat in silence, Jan lay unconscious on his back, his head in a widening halo of red, and Adrian, a few feet away, propped himself on one arm and cried continually, 'Why doesn't someone help me?'

Adrian's wounds looked the grimmest, and it was obvious that none of us could help him in any substantial way. His forehead was visibly broken open and a sliver of skull bone seemed to project from it.

Sometimes I wonder whether I am as emotional as the average man. I have loved, hated, been sad, been frightened, but displays of emotion only seem to come on the most bizarre occasions. Once, on a stormy sea in mid-Mediterranean, the yacht I was on was slowly overtaken by a Dutch coaster also heading towards Malta. The sense of the camaraderie of the sea as we exchanged cheerful hoots and dipped ensigns to each other filled my eyes with tears. Even a fast diesel train hurtling through Surbiton station can cause a strange upwelling of the spirit. And yet as I looked, almost dispassionately, at the battered bodies of my friends on the snow I felt only a detachment, a deadness, a matter-of-fact acceptance. I suppose this was partly the result of shock: the full realization of what had happened was to be borne in on me later.

'Can you somehow rig this arm up?' I asked Nick, and he began to rummage around in his rucksack. I hoisted up my wrist and soon Nick had attached a sling.

Before I left I remember dismissing as callous and inappropriate the thought which had flashed across my mind, that one of us should take some photographs of the general scene and of the individual wounded. As I dismissed it I also remember thinking that we would later come to regret the omission.

'I'll get on down, then, and get some help up to you,' I said, moving off after Peter, whose distant orange anorak I could just make out as he plunged down a lava gully.

Nick watched us with mixed feelings as we both disappeared. Even with broken arms it would probably only take us an hour or two to reach the base camp and alert Gerardo and the two porters. They would have heard the eruption and would clearly have realized from the timing of it that we had been caught up in it. Perhaps they had already set out with a tent, a stove and some food.

It was a gloriously sunny day. Nick sat on the snow and his initial feelings of self-pity quickly gave way to a sense of gratitude at his survival with no broken bones. Around him were three grim examples of the less lucky: Jan once tried

Alao, the village
at our roadhead
and the domain of
Don Alfonso
Merino

At Licto an
Indian mother
spins as she sits
waiting for a bus

Alao's main street.

Nick, the author and
Jan confer outside the
rest-house there

Jan decided to move from Alao to Guarguallá, over the col (centre) in the next valley to the south.

Don Alfonso's son Fausto (in the sheepskin chaps) owned this valley. In front of his hacienda his wife and daughter greet one of Haroun Tazieff's Ecuadorean soldiers and Gerardo Herrera, our Ecuadorean geologist, while three peons look on

Our four guides – Ramón, Anacleto, the boy and Callisto –
constantly had to stop to adjust the mules' loads

At Plaza Pamba the animals could go no further. Jan watches
Gerardo write a letter for the guides, arranging our later
rendezvous with them

to stand up but collapsed on all fours. Nick spoke to him but he was too deeply concussed to hear; Adrian continued to cry for help, whilst Ron, his breathing laboured and heavy, seemed also to have sustained a severe skull fracture and to have little chance of living.

Nick returned to Adrian, whose likelihood of survival seemed the most precarious of all, took a sleeping bag out of his rucksack and with great difficulty got him into it and zipped him up. Jan, in a deep coma now, was breathing low but normally and his pulse was strong. Despite a deep gash in the top of his skull he seemed to be the most hopeful prospect of the three. Nick managed to put him into a big, orange, polythene survival bag.

After half an hour he again went over to Ron, who now appeared to be dead. He checked his heart-beat but there was nothing there. He stood over him and said a prayer. He recalled Ron's self-sacrifice, his enthusiasm for the expedition, his courage in fighting acclimatization problems, his determination to get to the top of Sangay. Ron had not yet been a week in Ecuador. Nick remembered that Ron had a wife, Jeannine, and a daughter, Chelsea. Little consolation to them to know that Ron had perhaps proved himself in the end as a fully-fledged expeditioneer, caught fatally at 16000 feet by monstrous ill fortune.

Returning to Jan and Adrian, Nick began to pull them together and Adrian, in his pain, set up a great caterwauling. 'Leave me alone!' he cried, but eventually they were centralized and Nick sat down between them. Every now and then he blew his whistle to guide any possible help towards him. 'What a perfect day for flying!' he thought, but at the same time knew it was days too soon to expect air rescue.

The afternoon was a sort of purgatory. First Jan and then Adrian would thrash about and tear themselves out of their bags and fling themselves sliding down the slope, the shiny synthetic material offering little resistance on the ice. He had no hope of dragging an inert body back up and so would draw the other down to keep them together and then climb back up the snow on his rapidly stiffening leg to collect the rucksacks and other gear. Adrian continually called for water and then tried to struggle out of his bag to pee. As Nick pulled his trousers up and tried to settle him again, Jan began to wriggle sideways preparatory to setting off downhill once more. This slow, involuntary descent went on from one outcrop of lava to another until evening came.

As the sun went down beyond the Chimborazo massif Nick still fully expected help to come from the base camp. Why had no rescue party yet arrived? He agonized over the possible reasons for this delay. The two survivors were becoming restive, and he had to decide whether to stay with them all night or go down to the base camp himself. Selflessly, he decided to stay.

About one o'clock Peter Chadwick had set off down the snow at a fast clip, falling over several times in his haste. Three or four minutes later, one arm tightly slung, I had followed him, but he soon disappeared from my sight altogether. He had visions of getting down to Gerardo and the porters in very quick time and, not appreciating yet the extent of the damage Sangay had caused, he imagined them quite soon up with Nick and being able to help the wounded walk down the mountain back to the base camp.

Peter was soon below the snowline and stumbling down a lava ridge which he took to be the one that we had toiled up in the morning. When I reached this point myself I began to wonder why I had not seen any of our orange marker flags. At first I surmised that they had been knocked away by falling rocks, but soon it dawned on me that the volcanic *ejecta* had not reached as far down as this and that we were, in fact, on a different lava ridge.

'Peter, we're too far south,' I shouted. 'We've got to get over these ridges to our right.'

'Yes!' came an answering call from far below me.

I've always had a highly developed directional sense, and have wandered through places like Marseilles, Tel Aviv, Kingston (Jamaica), Harar, without failing to get back to hotel or railway station (Teheran's boring gridiron plan is the only one so far to throw me). The same built-in compass seems to work in the wild, too, and although mist and high ridges hid base camp from view I sensed, rightly, that the eruption had knocked us down Sangay's flank on a line about 15 degrees off the mean course of our ascent, and that Peter and I ought to have headed much more north-westerly down the mountain.

Now, for the second time, I felt that things were going seriously wrong. I tried to climb up the slope to my right but near the ridge I slipped and fell flat on the greasy surface. Tantalizingly, I could not quite reach with my extended left arm the sharply eroded edge of the ridge by which I could have pulled myself over it. I was like a one-armed cat-burglar slithering over wet roof tiles. A false move and I would have slid thirty yards or so down the rain-smoothed slope.

Somehow I edged to safety and got over at another point. I managed to clear another similar mud arête, and Peter was doing the same perilous thing further down.

I felt I might now be on a better line of descent, and in a gulley bottom where the first tufts of grass began to appear I noticed some melt-water trickling down in the form of a small stream. I remembered the old adage that if you follow running water down a mountain it will generally get you off it. At first this seemed to be the answer and I found Peter's boot-marks, which was comforting. More bellowing confirmed that he was still down below me.

But Peter was in trouble of a different kind now. The stream had begun to plunge over small waterfalls and the gulley was closing in to become a steep-sided ravine of compacted mud, thickly clad in grasses and shrubs. By closing his right eye he could see clearly enough, but could not judge the height of the waterfalls. He jumped down several that were up to fifteen feet high and crashed down heavily onto the rocks below, his fractured arm flapping uselessly. He became frenzied as he seemed willy-nilly to be dropping into a ghastly trap.

Ultimately he came to the brink of a fall where the stream spouted twenty or thirty feet into a deep pot. There was no way of climbing down and looking behind him he realized that he could not get back up. Peter cursed his lot: Sangay, not content with blasting him off its sides, had now contrived for him this fiendish system of ravines. He cried out for help, but base camp was over a mile to the north and the only answering call came from me, far above him in a parallel valley.

He warned me of the pitfalls ahead, but I was already too deep into the same trap. Gingerly edging over waterfalls on my backside I came to a similar big chute. Descent was impossible and, like Peter, I saw no hope of clawing a way back up. I stood dazed on the black volcanic stream bed and watched the chill water trickle round my boots. I already felt weary and my right sleeve was now tacky with blood. There, like Man Friday's print in the sand, was Peter's boot-mark again. Where had he gone? If he had got clear, then I must be able to. The near-vertical bank on my right was the only possibility, and taking a handful of grass in my left hand I began to kick my way upwards. Infinitely laboured progress took me thirty or forty feet up. A fall backwards would probably have ended it all, but I somehow kept my balance and, after many long rests, came out on the top of a ridge.

All around me was a maze of green spurs plunging chaotically down towards the main river we called the Vulcan. The one I was on seemed to drop away immediately to the junction of two streams, so it was all to do again. I clambered down and began another agonizing haul up the farther side.

Peter, meanwhile, was facing his third or fourth almost sheer wall of loose earth. For this one he had to abandon his rucksack, with its cine-camera, film and survival bag. Thus lightened he was just able to scratch his way up the wall and reach the crest of the ridge.

The afternoon was wearing on now and Peter, seeing another chasm open up in front of him, began to despair of ever getting clear of the maze. 'If I'm benighted,' he thought to himself, 'I'll just tear up grass from the surrounding tussocks and lie under it for warmth.'

Similar notions filled my mind. At least twice, sitting totally enfeebled at the top of a ridge, I felt that all was up. How stupid to imperil my life in this way when I had escaped the volcano's wrath at mid-day! Thoughts of my other expeditions flitted through my head. This one was not at all like any of the previous seven or eight. Tragedy, black and howling, had never really struck before with such thoroughness. I suppose it was as wet as the three weeks in the Blue Mountains of Jamaica had been in 1973-4, but much colder and danker. My other ventures had all offered quite different hazards. I had come through numerous spills in the white water of the upper Blue Nile and the Zaire Rivers, and in north-west Ethiopia I had twice been shot at by gangs of bandits. But the dangers there had been sudden and short-lived and were mitigated by the presence of many good friends, at the peak of their fitness and strengthened by high morale and newly forged bonds of expedition comradeship.

Now I was with a broken band – half of the team on the brink of death, the remainder maimed, debilitated and alone. I was at a very low ebb.

Cloud still filled the distant valleys but as I sat slumped amid the wet tussocks a gap suddenly appeared in it to the northwards and on a sepia berg about a mile away I saw the two orange tents of the base camp.

This electrifyingly hopeful piece of good luck brought me to my feet.

'*Ayuda!*' I bellowed at the top of my voice. '*Venga, Gerardo! Venga por nosotros! Ayuda!*'

My cries seemed to carry over the desolate, still terrain, and I was overjoyed to see two tiny figures spill out of the tents and start scurrying about on the lava.

Five hours had now passed since the eruption and Gerardo and Anacleto, roused by my shouts, began to make their way up the main river. They were only a few hundred yards from the camp when they found Peter stumbling along the stream bed.

'Jan is very badly hurt and Richard and I have broken arms,' he blurted out. 'Richard's up there where I've just come from.'

'OK, we take you back,' said Gerardo.

But Peter said, 'No, go up for Richard,' and staggered on down until he reached the big lava berg.

As he was climbing up it a strange hallucination appeared on a high grassy ridge to his left. He thought he could hear shouts and believed he could quite clearly see Nick, Ron, Adrian, Gerardo and the guides carrying Jan and running away down the valley. He thought they were calling out for him to join them, and he started jogging after them back down the lava flow away from the camp, shouting to them as he went. But they seemed to be leaving him behind at an alarming rate and as it was almost evening he decided to turn and make for the tents, spend the night there alone and catch them up in the morning.

Gerardo and Anacleto thrust up into the maze of ravines and soon I saw them surmount a ridge a few hundred yards away. I shouted at them and then sank back amid the tussocks with an ineffable sense of deliverance.

Minutes later they were manhandling me down the steep slopes, Anacleto leaping about with the surefootedness of a chamoix, tearing shrubs out of our path and kicking steps for me with his heels. With every plunging step downwards the bones in my right arm crepitated, and it was with intense relief that I reached the river bank and was hauled slowly along it.

In the gathering dusk, some five and half hours after I had set off down, we came to the foot of the lava berg. Here an astonishing sight confronted us. Toiling up the river bed was a party of about a dozen Ecuadorean Indians, dressed in climbing gear and hung about with ropes. They were the spearhead of Haroun Tazieff's French expedition, though (in my shock and exhaustion) I did not at first realize it.

Immediately I tried to urge them to get up the mountain to where Nick and the others lay on the snow. With mounting hysteria I explained the gravity of our plight, but the Ecuadoreans just stood mutely and stared at me with all the impassivity of their race. I became angry and stormed at them in broken Spanish for their hardness of heart. I threatened them that their president would be informed of their fecklessness. I turned to cajoling them and offered them large sums of money (which I did not have) in return for an immediate rescue bid. All to no avail.

In retrospect it was understandable. They had marched many miles throughout a long day. No Indian ever relishes climbing the slopes of Sangay even by day. It would be dark before they got anywhere near our wounded friends. And in any case they were not mountain men but simple peasants from distant valley farmsteads. '*Mañana por la mañana*,' they said, and so I had to admit defeat and accept their undertaking to go up early the next day.

Despondently I was led up the berg to our tents, where I found that Peter had collapsed in utter fatigue. The oncoming Ecuadoreans had clearly been the explanation for his imagined chain of figures running and shouting on a nearby ridge.

I told Gerardo all I could of the disaster on the mountain, and as I fell back into a troubled sleep I saw him making copious notes and writing instructions for anyone who might reach us after he had gone (see Appendix B). For privately, he had made a courageous decision; the only decision, in fact, that could save our shattered team, lacking a radio as we did. Gerardo decided that he would set off back on foot to Guargualla and the Land-Rover, and drive to Riobamba and the nearest telephone. He selected three of Tazieff's Indian vanguard as companions and at 2 a.m. while Peter and I, alongside one another, slept oblivious, he went off into the black night on his crucial long march.

7
Night on a Bare Mountain

It was a strange, rather frightening place. By day the lava
blocks . . . looked like dull, black coke. But at night these
glowed a rich cherry red as they rattled and rumbled down
the slope. Every few hours there was an eruption from the
main crater. We could not see anything, for the entire
summit was wrapped in cloud.

Chris Bonington, *The Next Horizon*

Of all the many varieties of volcano Sangay is described as
Strombolian. Like its prototype in the Mediterranean it sits
quietly and exudes gases from vents and fumaroles on its
sides, discharging from time to time plumes of white steam
or black, ash-laden clouds; then with alarming suddenness
and no warning earth tremor it will vomit high into the sky
a mass of fragmented, pyroclastic rocks from its inner core.
These fall back down, a few dropping again into the three
craters on the summit, the rest glancing off its shoulders
and cannonading down the mountain's sides with terrifying
velocity.

Bonington describes Sangay as having erupted as many
as 400 times in one day and Peter Francis, our volcanologist,
has called it 'the highest, most consistently active volcano
in the world'. He adds that it is certainly the most consistently active of all the hundreds of volcanoes in the entire
length of the Andes.

But was there ever, we wondered, any pattern to this
activity? This was to be an object of our future study.
From our researches we did not know of any such pattern,

and we had not ourselves been long enough yet in the vicinity of the mountain to establish if there was one.

Edward Whymper, wood engraver, celebrated Alpinist, conqueror of the Matterhorn, came to tackle the great Andes in Ecuador in 1879. From his Camp Three, 17285 feet up Chimborazo, he and Louis Carrel watched Sangay erupt several times:

It appeared to be distant from us about forty miles, and its rather symmetrical cone rose well above the intervening ranges. There were large snow-beds near its summit, but the apex of the cone was black, and was doubtless covered in fine volcanic ash. The saying is current that eruptions of Sangai are to be apprehended when Cotopaxi becomes tranquil, and the opinion seemed to prevail that the two mountains act as safety-valves to each other.

What Whymper describes as 'outrushes of steam' occurred every twenty or thirty minutes, shooting up with great rapidity some 5–6000 feet above Sangay and forming a mushroom-like cloud which the wind blew ten or twelve miles to the south before it was dissipated.

Whymper was never to climb Sangay – it was too far from the mainstream of classic Ecuadorean volcanoes – but his careful observations noted that about 4000 feet of the mountain was visible to him and that the 'steam' rose up to one and a half times this height in less than three seconds – a speed of about 1320 mph.

There was a clear pattern of activity here, of some fifty to seventy eruptions every twenty-four hours. But a hundred years later things had clearly changed. Neither Dyott, nor Moore, nor Lewis and Estill report any such continuous activity, and Bonington and Snow in 1966 found Sangay much less volatile. We had heard an eruption on the evening of 9 August. The mountain had slumbered throughout the 10th and 11th but had blown again at noon on the 12th.

Yet it was still reputed to be very active. As dusk fell on its snowy flanks Nick must have wondered if it might blow again. He lay between Jan, who was on an exposed shoulder of ash, and Adrian, stretched out in a sleeping bag with a

polythene sheet around his head and upper arms. Still Nick
hoped that someone from base camp would come up with
a tent to put over them. As it got darker and colder he
knew he had eleven hours of night to survive.

Jan kept flicking and twisting himself about and so Nick
held on to him firmly with one hand. With the other he
wrapped a piece of polythene round himself to keep some
of the wind out. He lay staring up at the heavens and
watched the Milky Way, the Great Bear and the Southern
Cross revolve slowly round the night sky.

Halfway through the night Adrian, who never ceased
crying out in his anguish, slid away into the darkness. Nick
thought that it would perhaps be to a merciful release. To
prevent the same happening to Jan, Nick moved from
above him to wedge himself like a chock underneath him.
And the bitter wind blew down Sangay's slopes so that for
long spells Nick had to thump his boots up and down and
squirm and jiggle about on the snow to keep the blood
going round. Jan could not move like this, so Nick constantly ensured that he was still lying on his green karrimat
with his head on a rucksack, so that he did not lose too
much body warmth into the ground. Despite this the ends
of his toes were badly frostbitten.

As night limped slowly away the wind tugged at the
flapping sheets of polythene and they began to fray and
disintegrate. Nick dozed fitfully but what he thought about
in between times he has not revealed. Occasionally he blew
his whistle and flashed his torch towards base camp.

Friday the 13th dawned beautifully and Nick's abiding
memory is of the magnificent dome of Chimborazo, Queen
of the Andes, floating sunlit above the clouds forty-seven
miles to the north-west. To the south, the serrated, snow-
clad edge of a part of the cordillera scintillated in the sun's
first rays, the rim of an extinct volcano perhaps, with no
smoke pall above it. Nick wondered why we had not chosen
something like that to climb instead of the fuming giant
behind him, whose single cough had flung us into disorder
and ruin.

Rescue must surely come now and Nick waited an hour or two with mounting expectations of the distant shout, the glimpse of a bright anorak against the lower snow slopes. Instead, he saw Adrian about 300 feet below, where he had come to rest on a shoulder of lava. As Nick stood up and unbent his limbs and began to collect together the scattered bits and pieces of kit, Jan's body, now without its human prop, slid slowly down the ice towards Adrian.

Nick went down and dragged Jan closer to his dear friend and found that Adrian, miraculously, was still alive. He then centralized the gear around the two supine forms and tried to warm them both a little and tuck them more tightly into their sleeping bags. He decided then that as it was 7 a.m. and no rescue had come it was up to him to go and get it.

Rescue, in fact, was on its way. Tazieff's Ecuadorean guides, true to their word, had risen early and set off up the mountain. They climbed by the route that we had all taken on the previous days and must have been getting near to the little cluster of bodies when Nick, having laid out the long climbing rope on the snow as a marker and tied Jan and Adrian together to secure them from any further downhill glissading, strode off down the nearest gulley. By a tragic irony Nick saw what he took to be an orange flag, but it was in fact a tattered fragment of Jan's survival bag, and so he made the same directional error as Peter and me, and thus missed the posse of guides by taking a too southerly route into the maze of ravines.

Nick could see no recognizable landmark. The snow was grey with ash. Patches of black cinders were everywhere, and rocks, plate-sized and larger, were buried a foot or more where they had landed the day before. He pondered the madness of it all.

An added hazard soon faced him: the smooth, wet shoulders of lava mud that Peter and I had slithered and fallen on were now iced over. Crossing them was like scaling a giant Pear Hélène. His legs repeatedly shot away from under him. Soon he reached the more steeply flanked valleys with their tussock grass and scrub – and began to follow an infant stream down its course.

Repeatedly, sheer waterfalls forced him away from the stream and up the sides of the ravine – vertical for the first few yards, then near-vertical. With four sound limbs he managed them more competently than Peter Chadwick and me, but it was cruel work. From time to time he collapsed on a ridge top and breathed in the scents of the herbage around him, re-establishing some sort of contact with the natural world and trying to expunge from his mind the horrors of the preceding day and night.

After some moments stern reality would reassert itself.

'If I don't get to that base camp and get some sort of help to them,' he would say to himself, 'then all those boys up there will die.'

Nick somehow got down to the upper Namaquimi River and found our boot-prints. Forging northwards he had to wade it frequently. There must have been many an echo of the Himalayas for this Gurkha officer as he thrashed through the ice-cold melt-water. Soon he came to the familiar lava berg and hacked his way about sixty-five feet up a crumbling couloir onto the top. When the orange tents came into view he blew on his whistle and Ramón came scampering down towards him. Gratefully he handed over his rucksack and came slowly up to the camp.

'Hello, Nick,' Peter and I said feebly from our sleeping bags as he stuck his head between the tent flaps.

News was quickly exchanged.

'Don't for Chrissake reproach yourself for taking the wrong route down,' I said. 'All those ridges of lava look the same. Anyway, you didn't take nearly six hours the way we did.'

'Very nearly,' he said. 'But I wonder if Anacleto and those other guides will find Jan and Adrian?'

'Sure they will. Come and have some of Ramón's excellent boiled carrots.'

Nick first took a draught of cold water and then shared our simple lunch. Since breakfast thirty hours earlier he had

managed on half a bar of chocolate and three boiled
sweets.

Peter lay morose and thoughtful at the news of his great
friend Ron's death. I mused, too, on the unfairness of it all:
Ron had put so much into the expedition, in his quiet,
unassuming way. To be a part of it had probably meant
more to him than it had to any of us, and now he was the
first to go. We quizzed Nick closely on the state of Jan and
Adrian, the gravity of whose wounds Peter had somehow
not appreciated. It was a grim account.

But during it a faint noise on the lava heralded the return
of the rescue party. Nick dashed out expectantly. Peter and
I lay and waited and did not understand the significance of
his silence followed by a disconsolate 'Oh, no!'

They had come back empty-handed.

'*Sí, Patrón*, we found them,' said one, 'and two *señores* are
still alive. But they were too heavy to lift.' They had put Jan
into a sleeping bag.

Nick somehow contained his anger, paid them 100 sucres,
told them to make a second effort during the afternoon
and dismissed them to get their lunch – spaghetti and more
carrots.

Not long afterwards seven of them set off again with our
second tent which Nick had taken down and given them to
put over Jan and Adrian if they still could not be moved.
They carried a stove to warm the air in the tent. But their
urgent instructions were to bring the two survivors down
as fast as possible.

As the afternoon passed we pondered on our chances of
rescue.

'Gerardo will most likely have met Tazieff's team coming
in,' said Nick, who had stationed himself in the mouth of
our tent. 'He's got a twenty-strong Ecuadorean army
support group with him and they'll get through to Riobamba on their radio.'

It seemed reasonable and as we lay with the sun dappling
the orange material above us Peter and I listened with some
confidence for a helicopter.

By and by, distant shouts came from the ravine beyond the tents, into which dropped our route to Sangay. The guides were back. Nick picked up the rope, which they had recovered on their first trip, and ran the two hundred yards to the edge of the berg.

Down below him was an exhausted bunch of guides carrying two bodies on their shoulders. Nick's lowered rope was lashed round the first one and the Ecuadoreans manhandled it carefully up the precipitous wall. The second came up in good style and Nick helped in the final carry back to the tents.

'*Muchas gracias! Muchas gracias!*' he said, and indicated that they would be paid again. The gallant boys who had borne these awkward burdens over such difficult terrain nodded shyly. It couldn't have been an easy trip.

As they laid the bodies gently down Nick's gratitude and relief was chilled by another numbing tragedy: he looked at Adrian, blue-lipped and no longer breathing, and found that his heart had stopped. Somewhere on the jolting descent his seemingly indomitable spirit had given up. Nick covered the battered head and face, now in quiet repose, and zipped the sleeping bag right up.

He came to the tent and said, 'I'm afraid Adrian's gone.'

Although, in the light of his wounds, this was hardly a surprise, the news jolted us both severely. And it was now my turn for special grief.

Adrian had in some sense been my protégé. As an awkward officer-cadet at Sandhurst, often in trouble, he had come to my quarters by way of escape, to talk expeditions. His first venture had been as a cadet with Jan and me to southern Ethiopia in 1972. Seized by the lure of wild places, absorbed by the contrasts to formal military life which expeditions offer and fascinated by nature in all its forms – rocks, plants, animal life – he gave himself over to scientific exploration and collection. A second venture in Ethiopia aborted but he found himself with me again in Harley Nott's expedition to the Blue Mountains of Jamaica in

1973–4. Here his industry and self-denial made him a superlative quartermaster and he collected botanical specimens for Caroline Whitefoord of the British Museum (Natural History). The splendid isolation of our site and the camaraderie of Harley's fifteen-strong team had a visible emotional effect on Adrian. This was the only life.

Somehow I seemed to have pointed the way for him, and so after he had had difficulties with officialdom in planning his own follow-up expedition to the Jamaican Cockpit Country it seemed natural that he should get a last-minute place on the Zaire River Expedition, about which he had heard so much from me throughout 1974.

And now he had been re-united with Jan, Peter, Ron and me in our climbing enterprise in Ecuador. Although it was terrible for death to come so cruelly early in his life, it was perhaps a moment that he would have suggested was appropriate.

Caroline Whitefoord once heard Adrian quote with evident approval these lines from Don Marquis's *archy and mehitabel*, from the poem 'the lesson of the moth':

> we get bored with the routine
> and crave beauty
> and excitement
> fire is beautiful
> and we know that if we get
> too close it will kill us
> but what does that matter
> it is better to be happy
> for a moment
> and be burned up with beauty
> than to live a long time
> and be bored all the while . . .
> . . . it is better to be a part of beauty
> for one instant and then choose to
> exist than to exist forever
> and never be a part of beauty
> our attitude towards life
> is come easy go easy

we are like human beings
used to be before they became
too civilized to enjoy themselves

And now, like Archy's moth, Adrian had immolated himself in Sangay's fires.

8

In the Lap of the Gods

Come not between the dragon and his wrath.
King Lear, I, i, 121

Evening was coming upon us and when Nick Cooke asked
the guides if they would go up a third time and bring down
Ron Mace's body they naturally demurred. So Nick turned
his attentions to Jan, whom he had now installed in the
drier of our two tents.

'How's he doing, Nick?' I asked.

'Well, he's much the way he was on the mountain.
Regular heart-beat, regular breathing, but deeply unconscious.'

Nick did not elaborate on Jan's condition, so as not to
distress us. In truth, his wounds were absolutely ghastly.
A big rock had struck him on the crown of the head,
splitting his skull like a ripe pumpkin. Where the blow
had fallen his cranium had been stove in about an inch and
wide fissures had opened up towards his neck and over the
top of his head to the bridge of his nose.

'I daren't monkey about with his wounds,' Nick said,
'in case I put more infection in than I can clean out.'

Nor did he dare give him food or drink in case he choked
on it in his unconsciousness. Jan was left to fight the battle
himself with whatever inner reserves he had. We just hoped
and prayed he could survive until our relief came.

Doubts and apprehensions began to creep in among us
as darkness fell.

D

'D'you think they've begun to mount a rescue for us?' Peter asked.

'I expect the Mañana Principle will operate here as elsewhere in Latin America,' was my jaundiced comment.

'It *is* still Friday the thirteenth, you know,' Nick added. In fact, Gerardo, who had left on foot at 2 a.m. that same morning, had shown amazing fortitude and covered the fifteen miles to the Hacienda Guarguallá in fourteen hours – a journey that had taken us two and a half days on the way in. He had broken into the Land-Rover, driven as fast as he dared over the hair-raising track to Riobamba and from the nearest telephone had spoken to his superiors at the Department of Geology and Mines in Quito.

Dr Jeff Aucott of the British Geological Mission was at El Pub Inglés having a few beers with members of the Los Tayos Expedition. Friday the thirteenth had been a bad day for him, too: a big hassle in the morning over some paperwork, then a message from a team out in the field that one of his geologists had fallen into a ravine and broken a rib. About 7.30 p.m. he was called to the El Pub phone. Cupping his hand over his unengaged ear, he heard the voice of his Ecuadorean boss, Ingeniero Carlos Mosquera.

'I heard just now from Gerardo Herrera in Riobamba. Your expedition to the volcano Sangay has had an accident. He says that there has been an eruption. Two men are hurt and four are missing.'

Jeff immediately called the British defence attaché, Group-Captain Peter Wills, who was dining with the Nicaraguan ambassador. Plans were made to inform the Ecuadorean authorities, the army and the air force, straight away.

So at the very moment of growing gloom in base camp, arrangements were being set in train in Quito which were to lead – after many difficulties and delays – to our ultimate recovery.

Contributing to the spread of gloom was the close presence, just outside on the lava, of Adrian's corpse, and of the more distant but just as poignant presence of Ron's, up there on the mountain. As I lay and listened to the wind

I could not help but speculate on that eternal question: why was I in my sleeping bag, warm and alive, while they were gone? As I had been sliding down the snow face I had more than half expected a rock to strike my head and a great, black oblivion to fill it. But here I was – conscious, sentient, mentally alert.

Nick retired to his sleeping bag in Jan's tent and Peter Chadwick and I settled down in ours. The rain began to patter on its orange sides and as there was no fly-sheet we had to be careful not to touch the thin fabric as we moved. This was not too difficult as movement was so painful. I lay on my back with my right arm now fully extended by my side. Any slight shift and the shattered end of the humerus would grind against the heads of the radius and the ulna, which had been turned over by the impact like the tops of two old crow-bars.

'Pass the bottle,' I said to Peter.

'In or out?' he asked.

We had two plastic bottles, one full of fresh river water, the other to pee into. At night it was important to be certain which of them one picked up.

A severe shock seems to interrupt some of the body's natural functions, we discovered. Although we regularly filled the pee bottle neither of us felt any other inner stirrings. Whether it was our wounds or the prospect of crawling painfully out into the consistently evil conditions, I do not know; but our trousers were never lowered until we got into the Vozandes Hospital in Quito.

Our tents soon became rather stale and fetid. Next morning I realized that my wound must be a contributory factor.

'I wonder if you could bear to put some dressings on our arms,' I asked Nick after we had had some breakfast tea, 'mine's beginning to heave pretty horribly.'

'I've got no special medical expertise,' he protested.

'Never mind,' I assured him, 'you must have done the course at some time. Anyway, I'm not asking for a tonsillectomy. Just slap something on to stop it leaking into my sleeve.'

I had not dared to take off my green anorak in case, so my wild imaginings ran, the arm fell apart. In the event it was not so dramatic.

'Ramón! *Agua!*' shouted Nick, pointing at the cooking stove.

Ramón's curiously Chinese features were set sourly. As they struggled from their nest of damp grasses under the sagging nylon sheet, he and Anacleto must have felt that life was not at its cheerfullest. However, he took an empty pan and disappeared down a well-worn path to the nearby stream.

In a little while Nick had the water bubbling merrily. He wanted to clean his hands and to try and get the scissors and tweezers in the first-aid pack something like sterile.

With some difficulty I took my anorak off, but when he had sized up the situation Nick said, 'Don't bother about your shirt.'

He reached for the scissors and began to cut the right sleeve off at the shoulder. It was a World War Two vintage khaki shirt and the coarse material was blackened with dried blood.

Nick patiently cut it all away until he was left with a small tuft over the wound itself. Fortunately, as this was on the outside of my arm, which was now swollen like a pork sausage, I could not see that a sharp point on the boulder had driven the shirt actually *into* my arm.

Nick said nothing but just dabbed away with lint and boiling water. It was painful, but in a little while he was able to take hold of the tuft and slowly pull it out. Somehow it felt better.

'Who's got the shell dressing?' Nick asked.

'I don't know,' I said. 'I know we have one.'

Peter started to rummage in the pockets of his rucksack. 'Not here,' he stammered.

Many is the time I have taken a shell dressing with me on some trip – 'just in case someone falls off a cliff' – and never used one yet. Nick searched around outside for some time. Now we actually wanted one it could not be traced. Its familiar, stitched up wrapper of faded cotton – 'War Office – Army Medical Department – SHELL DRESSING – Cuxson, Gerrard & Co. Ltd., Oldbury, October 1944' – could not be found anywhere. So Nick had to make do with a tiny square of lint and thin strips of sticking plaster.

I found some antibiotic tablets in the medical pack, took a couple, and settled down to watch Nick get to work on Peter.

In an attempt to stop himself careering down the icy slopes of Sangay Peter had dug his arms and legs into the snow. In so doing he had ripped off some quite large patches of skin. These areas were pitted with lava ash and general grime and were beginning to suppurate nastily. It was delicate work, and not easy for Peter, but Nick managed to clean him up quite well and apply some bandages.

Then the final touch. Nick felt that to stop Peter moving and hurting himself he should attach some splints. But we had nothing suitably rigid and no wood grew within miles. However, after an exhaustive search around the camp Anacleto came back with four pieces of twig which Nick hopefully bound onto Peter's upper arm.

'Squirrel Patrol is proud of you,' I said. 'Remind me to give you your doctor badge when we get back.'

Some of Tazieff's Ecuadorean guides had come up to our camp and stood around the tents in the thin drizzle. Occasionally a bolder spirit would move nearer and peer through the tent flaps at the wounded gringos. I got into conversation with some of them but despite my entreaties the rain and rising winds deterred them from going up the mountain to bring down Ron's body. However, Nick wrote a brief message and, working on the Belt and Braces Principle, we decided to ask three of them to take it out to Riobamba. Something untoward might, after all, have happened to Gerardo. We did not know, and it was safer to be double-banked. A boy of sixteen or so with an unusually sunny smile took the note from me. It had rather more specific details about our condition. He and his companions set off, met the French party on its way in,

and quite quickly reached Guarguallá. I later learned that
he was called Angel Huambo – entirely suitably for one who
bore tidings if not good, at least better than Gerardo's
original news.

The tidings might have been even better if our Angel had
waited a few moments longer.

'What was that?' I asked suddenly, propping myself up
on the left elbow. 'I thought I heard a moaning noise.'

Nick crawled out and into the tent which immediately
faced ours.

'It's Jan!' he cried. 'I think he's coming to!'

Jan's lips fluttered and another weak cry came from deep
within him. This was a great tonic. If he regained consciousness we might be able to give him some encouragement to
pull through. And it would be possible to feed him.

'Hey! That's marvellous!' said Peter.

'Yes,' I agreed, smiling. 'I know Jan too well. If he
wakes up now he'll have us all out there finishing off the
reconnaissance.'

I recalled to Peter the time in Ethiopia when Jan had
accidentally discharged his Browning pistol whilst riding
on the top of a lorry. The bullet had passed into his own
knee, out below it, into the instep of his right foot and out
again. It was found later in his sock. I had taken over the
running of the expedition, and we conveyed Jan as fast as
could be from a point near the Kenya border towards
Addis Ababa. Even from his stretcher as he lay in the back
of the jolting lorry he still tried to direct operations and
concerned himself with the logistic problems of the return
to the capital.

In fact, Jan did not emerge yet from his coma, but the
occasional moan showed us that the inner struggle was still
going on.

Confinement to a tent, perhaps like confinement in prison,
sharpens one's sense of hearing and heightens one's aware-
ness of the unseen, outside world. All conversation was
stilled when, late in the morning, we heard the unmistakable
cracks of a distant rifle. This was a mystery indeed. We were

deep in uninhabited land, though we knew hunters some-times penetrated this far east and in fact G. Edward Lewis reported in 1950, 'Game – deer, tapirs, pumas and rabbits – was unbelievably plentiful all around El Sangay.'

Nick called Anacleto over and we asked him to go off and see who it was and if possible bring them back to camp. After squatting on his haunches in the tent door for a while and grappling with my Spanish, he stood up and, though his blank, uncomprehending features never changed, soon plunged off down towards the river.

Steadily Nick prepared soup for lunch and handed in two mugs for Peter and me. It was towards the end of our siesta that we heard the scuff of boots on the lava. Suddenly the flap of the tent was pulled back and the bulk of an enormous man filled the entire entrance. He looked like Oliver Hardy in a drab green, US Army uniform, but it was Sargento Segundo Cadena of the Ecuadorean army's *Fuerzas Especiales*. Over his shoulder, almost but not quite a Stan Laurel, peered the thinner, pixie face of another soldier.

This was a great relief and very diverting. The first outsiders had reached us and so, we comforted ourselves, our rescue was beginning. They were members of Haroun Tazieff's army support group, from the *Brigada 'Patria' No. 1*, and had been foraging ahead with rifles and a dog in the hope of shooting some deer for the pot.

We gave the sergeant a mug of hot lemonade and he offered help. He addressed us as if we were at the far end of a Quito parade ground and his manner suggested that we were foolish but fundamentally honest recruits who had somehow failed him on a military exercise. I suppose sergeants the world over develop the notion that their fellow men are, by and large, feckless innocents whose understanding of an instruction is in proportion to the number of decibels with which it is given. This was Cabo II Didio Romero, he shouted, indicating the man behind him, and he was a medical orderly. He would come back later on with his equipment. Meanwhile we must be of good cheer. And with that they went.

Tazieff's expedition had reached the area and was pitching a camp about a mile to the north of us on a very large, flat lava berg that we had all crossed on our way in along the river valley four days before. The Ecuadorean army marches with minimal rations and Sergeant Cadena had been out looking for their supper when Anacleto found him. In the course of the afternoon Cabo II Didio Romero returned with several of his fellow corporals. On his left sleeve he had proudly tied a Red Cross armband and I have never in my life been so moved by the sight of Jean Henri Dunant's famous emblem. It seemed to represent all that we most needed first of all – some specialist care for Jan. As the corporals crowded round our tent and chatted, Didio organized boiling water and unwrapped his medical instruments.

Soon he disappeared into Jan's tent and was at work there for a long time. He carefully cut the hair around those dreadful wounds, cleaned them and applied some fairly strong antiseptic. This drew forth tremendous groans of pain from Jan but it could well have saved him. Didio and Nick then got Jan out of his sleeping bag and began to undress him. It was long past nappy-changing time. They dried him off and dressed him in some cleaner things. Later Didio even managed to give Jan some sips of orange juice into which he had ground up some antibiotic tablets. It was a valiant effort, requiring all the traditional patience of the nurse.

'It is not so bad,' he told us with a Fernandel grin. 'The head is broken but the brain is still inside. I expect he will live.' This prognosis cheered us no end.

Dusk descended and heavy rain came with it. A third, long, uncomfortable night lay ahead. Despite the day's excitements morale began to dip. Peter and I felt very feeble and turned to wondering again about the chances of getting away from Sangay.

Had we but known it, substantial steps had been taken in this direction. Peter Wills and Jeff Aucott in Quito had swung into action on the previous night. Jeff had gone round to Ingeniero Carlos Mosquera's house and from there had organized a four-man climbing team from the British community which was prepared to go in to Sangay overland. Their major lack was medical supplies and, in particular, blood – Gerardo had indicated that fresh blood would be needed for the injured.

Meanwhile, within an hour Peter Wills had spoken to the chief of staff of the Ecuadorean air force (FAE) and his director of operations. It took him another hour to discover that there were no serviceable helicopters in Quito, but he was assured that the FAE would provide an Alouette from Guayaquil the following morning, if one was available. On this understanding Jeff cancelled the British community's ground rescue plan.

Jeff had a final phone call early on Saturday morning from a young lecturer at the Polytechnic called Bernardo Baete, who had just reached Quito by car from Riobamba. Baete, a keen *andinista*, had been a liaison man with the French team when they had met Gerardo coming out. He had turned back to Riobamba to accompany the exhausted geologist, left him there to make the vital phone calls and pressed on to Quito. Now he was able to give Jeff useful information gleaned from Gerardo – for example, that the two injured were Snailham and Chadwick.

Having set things up for the morning Jeff and Peter Wills had collapsed in sleep at about 3 a.m. But they were up again at 6 a.m. Peter Wills's immediate concern was fuel for the Alouette. There was none in Riobamba and so it had to be procured in Quito and conveyed south by lorry. There is little inter-service cooperation in Ecuador, and it was left to Peter himself to find an army officer who could authorize a lorry. By 10 a.m. six 45-gallon drums were on their way out of Quito and by 4 p.m. the lorry had reached the camp of the *Brigada Blindada 'Galápagos' No. 1* at Riobamba, where, at noon, Captain Bolívar Agila and Lieutenant Carrasco had arrived in their Alouette III after a hazardous flight from Guayaquil over the windy *cordillera occidental*.

In mid-morning Jeff and Bernardo Baete had met Peter in his office at the British Embassy and a plan of action had been decided upon. As a result Jeff and Bernardo drove to Riobamba in a Department of Geology and Mines Land-Rover and were at the military camp at 2 p.m. It was a glorious, sunny day and had the fuel by then arrived Jeff thought that a rescue attempt might have been launched straight away. But Captain Agila had already made a tentative run towards Sangay, over country strange to him, and had gone up the wrong valley, where low cloud and deteriorating weather in the *cordillera oriental* had driven him back. So even when the fuel arrived he did not feel it wise to make another bid that evening.

Jeff outlined his plans to Major Jorge Andrade, the F A E officer coordinating our rescue from the Riobamba base, and had a final discussion with Gerardo Herrera, who was to stay in Riobamba and then guide Captain Agila to Sangay the next morning. Jeff and Bernardo then put a 45-gallon drum of aviation fuel in their Land-Rover and, in convoy with another, set off after nightfall on the circuitous, spine-jolting road up to the Hacienda Guarguallá. About 9.30 p.m. they were being entertained there by the laconic Señor Fausto Merino. The rescue operation, after twenty-four hours of urgent planning, was poised ready.

Meanwhile at Sangay our gloom was being relieved by some more friendly callers. Another memorably emotional moment came when we heard approaching voices and they turned out to be speaking French. The flaps parted to reveal three of Tazieff's scientists. Touchingly, they had brought some little delicacies for us – one a tin of condensed milk, the other a big bag of dried fruits ('*Frutas Secas . . . y Deliciosas*').

Peter Chadwick and I pierced the milk tin and took long, appreciative slugs at it. Never since my days at Oakham School had I enjoyed a similar indulgence so much. After lights in the Lower Twelve dormitory at Wharflands we would pass a tin of Nestlés from bed to bed.

'Hey, come on, it's my turn!'

'Shurrup, Dacombe!'

'We said it was sippers not gulpers.'

'That *was* a sip, honest, Glenn!'

I even remembered to tear off a semi-circle of the paper label for hygiene's sake.

When the Frenchmen left they had disappeared into the darkness to an accompaniment of rain and wind that was now approaching gale proportions. This made Nick's work doubly difficult. He had to prepare supper for five mouths (not including Jan's) and the stove was in the exposed space between the two tents. In bad weather – which seemed to mean almost always – he drew the stove into the mouth of a tent, which limited his mobility and needed constant vigilance.

Our food stocks, adequate for nine of us when we arrived at Sangay, seemed to have diminished dramatically. When Nick searched the rucksack there was barely anything left. However, he found two tins of goulash and some potato powder so he began to make what the army calls an all-in stew. A merger with the French seemed to be in view so he could afford to be reckless.

Gradually bubbles forced their way through to the top of the thick mixture. The smell, wafted by gusts of wind into our tent, caused Peter and me to grin foolishly like the two Bisto kids.

'Ramón! Anacleto!' shouted Nick across the few yards of lava, 'Dinner!'

There was no familiar acknowledgement, no movements in the darkness. Depressed no doubt by the torrential rain and their inadequate shelter, fearful of the mountain and homesick for their families, Ramón and Anacleto had stolen silently away. Nick knew their departure was imminent as they had asked to be released the previous day. He had persuaded them to stick it another twenty-four hours and paid them 800 sucres each – a hundred a day for eight days' work. Ironically, Gerardo, not knowing Nick had done this, later paid them the same amount over again!

We were abandoned now, and perhaps there was an explanation for our depleted food supplies. We cursed them, but our later reaction was to feel keenly for them in their long night march through a rising storm.

Nick brought the panful of steaming goulash into our tent and Peter and I levered ourselves awkwardly into a sitting position and sat there, mess tins at the ready, like a couple of cuckoos in the nest.

We were just about to tuck in when there was again a noise of tramping feet all around the tent. A hand drew back the door flap and we saw a powerful man, not unlike Omar Sharif, in a fluffy woollen hat and glistening black poncho from which the rain dripped liberally.

'Teniente Enrique Palacios, *Fuerzas Especiales*,' he said, introducing himself to Nick and shaking hands.

This presumably was the officer in command of Tazieff's support group, with some of his men gathered behind him.

'We come to bring you to our camp,' he said with military directness.

'What, now?' I asked, looking at the pan of goulash.

'Yes, now. Is important you come now.'

The storm howled and the rear of our tent, on the windward side, lifted momentarily in the air. The rain lashing the lieutenant's broad back sounded like a drum roll. Instinctively we all felt that now would not be the best moment to have to struggle out of our sleeping bags into the storm. How bitterly were we to regret our short-sightedness.

'Look,' said Nick, 'we're just about to have supper. It's our only real meal of the day. Could you come for us tomorrow?'

'If the helicopter come for you tomorrow, it come early in the morning when the weather is good,' said the lieutenant with relentless logic.

'We could be ready very early.'

'OK. We come for you at five.'

'OK.' This seemed reasonable and deferred the evil moment. The weather could be kinder then.

'OK. *Buenos noches!*' said the lieutenant and he and his men strode off into the rain.

'We couldn't have got Jan out in this,' said Peter, but in our hearts I think we all felt we'd taken the easy course.

Nick said, 'Come on, let's get some food inside us and get a good night's sleep.'

The stew was excellent and Peter and I followed it up with antibiotics and painkillers by way of dessert and collapsed back in our bags as if it was Christmas afternoon. Nick gave Jan some of the warm liquid and then settled down alongside him. They were both fairly dry, but our tent was extensively mottled now and rain ran copiously down the inside of it to collect in puddles on the sewn-in groundsheet. The wind now got up to a thin, high scream, like nymphets at an Osmonds concert. It tugged at the sagging roof but somehow the pegs seemed to be holding in the loose lava ash.

'You did remember to phone for an early call?' I asked Peter.

Before he could reply there was a noise which seemed even to still the banshee howl of the weather outside. A deep crack and rumble, like thunder but somehow more substantial, came from the mountainside above us. Sangay was in eruption again.

9
Low Ebb

Some say the world will end in fire,
Some say in ice.
Robert Frost, Fire and Ice

There was no knowing what scale of eruption it might be. Little and often is the Ecuadorean pattern now, according to Peter Francis. But in 1628 occurred Sangay's earliest recorded activity and there was nothing little about it then.

The proceedings of the city council of Riobamba for 3 November refer to

... the aforementioned city, upon which, about one month ago, the volcano of El Sangay, which lies towards the Province of Macas, burst asunder. And since the aforementioned time, it has thrown out enormous quantities of ash in this direction, which has spread out upon this district, blotting out the light of the sun and making the days dark, as it is this very day. Be it known that the city in general is terrorized, and that ... all the fields and pastures are covered with ash so that the cattle will not eat and are dying of hunger, and it is expected that if God, in His Divine Mercy, does not remedy the situation, most of the cattle will die, and this city and its inhabitants will be destroyed. ...

Riobamba is about thirty miles from Sangay and so the activity of October 1628, must have been exceptional.

As the violent booming reverberated above us in the night Peter Chadwick and I instinctively curled up in our sacks and covered our heads with our good arms.

'Christ, not again!' Peter murmured, and somehow also managed to lift his right arm up to protect his face.

But no rocks thudded down the slopes as far as our camp and so we slowly uncoiled. It was quite soon over and the rain and wind could dominate again.

Bravado soon crept back on stage.

'No problem there,' I said.

'No, nothing like Thursday.'

'In line with "Nurse of the Year" and "Goal of the Season" I vote ours "Eruption of the Week",' I added.

A kind of pattern was emerging: there had been explosive eruptions on the night of the 10th, at noon on the 12th and now on the night of the 14th – at present it seemed to be blowing about every two days.

I lay and pondered on this discovery, if discovery it was, as I waited for blessed sleep to overwhelm me. But as I awaited it the realization dawned that on this ill-starred night it probably never would. Peter and I had both for some time been edging into the middle of the tent to escape the rising tide but nevertheless large portions of my sleeping bag were now sodden. Only the area around my stomach seemed to have remained dry. Each movement produced a swish and suck of water and it was not long before the pair of us, like flood victims perched on an outhouse roof, were sitting up and leaning on each other back to back. In the other tent Jan spent most of the night flailing about with his left arm and thumping Nick, who eventually dragged his rucksack inside as a protective barrier.

The chill, damp night limped along and I suppose that at times we all dozed fitfully. Sleep, on these grim occasions, often comes in the early morning when the storm abates and a calm descends. Here, on Sangay, it did not work out that way. In the small hours the storm was at its worst, still violently buffeting all obstructions in its path.

'What do you make the time?' asked Peter.

'Just gone four-thirty. How are things?'

'Bloody terrible. I'm wet all through.'

'Me too. Never mind, eh? They'll be here soon.'

There was a faint noise from the other tent. By the light of a candle placed as far away as possible from Jan's left

arm Nick, like a guardsman on the retreat to Dunkirk, was
blacking and dubbining his boots. He next boiled his face
flannel, which had been employed the day before in cleaning
out Jan's head wounds and then mopping up his urine.
Nick had a perfunctory wash with it, borrowed Jan's
shaving gear and took off eight days' growth of beard. No
good looking scruffy in front of all these Frenchmen, he
thought. There was no doubting the good military sense of
having a thorough personal clean up in times of despair.
Clean shaven and with his boots neatly laced Nick felt
reinvigorated.

It was still pitch black when 5 a.m. came and Peter and I
listened intently for approaching footfalls. But there were
none. Six o'clock came, and the first glimmerings of light,
then seven. It wasn't much of a dawn. Heavy banks of grey
cloud still hung over us and the rain continued its diagonal
downpour.

'They're not coming, are they?'

'I can't see the helicopter coming in this either.'

This was *some* consolation.

'Have we anything to drink?'

Nick scratched about in the rucksack.

'Just custard powder and milk powder,' he said. 'Which
do you prefer?'

'I'd give anything for a fried egg,' said Peter.

As I sat and stared dumbly at my knees I saw the rich,
orange yolk and the spreading circle of white, crinkling
with brown now at the edges. With my left hand I thumped
my leg to drive the mirage away. Peter must have thought
I was cracking up. Ecuador is, I suppose, an appropriate
place to go bananas.

In the event Nick found a small tin of apple pudding and
brewed it up with the milk powder and the remains of the
condensed milk. After breakfast we sat about listlessly,
waiting for something to happen.

In the normal course of things I am kept fully occupied
on expeditions by the need to make notes of what goes on,
and I had handy in my pack three pocket-books marked

Nearing Sangay our
route began to cut
across the grain of
the country. Repeatedly
we dropped down
through *páramo* grass
to cross icy rivers and
climb again

Looking back over
the way we came to
the mountain. From
the closest ridge, near
the landslide (left), I
had a first glimpse of
Sangay (page 64) and
the lava bergs that lie
at its feet (foreground)

Sangay from the north with the eastern cordillera beyond

The recent lava spill on the northern flank with the current explosion crater above. We climbed the snow-field at far right

The three craters – the northern, presently dormant, the large central and the regularly active western, whose eruption of 12 August bombarded the team on the right-hand slopes

Minard Hall flew over the explosion crater a few days after the eruption (page 144)

Gerardo and Adrian make ready for the climb

At first we hacked up cold mud-ash strewn with pyroclastic rocks

Ecuador 1, Ecuador 2, Ecuador 3. Perhaps one per volcano, I had thought back at home in Camberley. Only *Ecuador 1* had begun to become dog-eared and grimy, and even here the lines of miniscule red biro stopped halfway down page twenty.

The march in to Sangay had been too physically taxing and action-packed to allow me to make any proper record and my account of our affairs ended with the collection of Ron and Peter from the *Orcoma*. In base camp on the second night I had jotted down some details of our first climb up the mountain, but this was as far as the narrative had gone.

There was so much that I wanted to write down and my head was racing with useful material, but it was too wearisome to attempt it left-handed. The name 'Angel Huambo' is written falteringly on one page and 'Bernardo Baete' on another. But this long stretch of enforced idleness produced little else, and I chafed at being thus disabled from doing what I came with the expedition to do.

'You know what it is that's holding them up?' said Nick.

I imagine that we had all been working on the answer to that since early dawn: rain had now been dinning down for thirty-six hours and the broad stream at the foot of the berg, which we had easily forded on our way in, was probably a raging torrent. And the French camp was on the other side of it.

'I expect they can't cross the river,' Peter said, stating what was obvious to us all.

It was a bitter, ironic truth. We could have got away from the mountain the previous evening but our own self-indulgence had made us postpone the rescue. Now the weather had turned the tables on us and we had effectively cut ourselves off from all French aid. Food stocks were dangerously low, our guides had fled, Jan was beginning to shiver and shudder with cold and damp, and the rain did not look like relenting. We were at our lowest ebb.

There seemed to be nothing that we could do. Peter and I had stiffened and weakened. The injury to the sacral region of my back, where a smaller rock had struck, had now

immobilized my left leg, and I did not relish the thought of
any kind of movement. We might be marooned where we
were for many days. Sebastian Snow in 1966 had written:
'It was raining non-stop and we decided to sit it out and
wait for a spell of fine weather. For three days and nights
we remained in our tent, alternately cursing the weather
and reading a single, battered copy of *Anna Karenina*.'
I normally never travel anywhere without at least a paperback, but for the sake of lightness I had, with the others,
jettisoned all reading matter during a purge in the Kennerleys' basement in Quito. I'd have given anything now
for some solid, time-consuming Tolstoy.

At 11 a.m. I saw Nick moving about in his tent. He had
already been out once or twice to tighten guy ropes or
replace pegs around a tent that now looked like a broken-
backed animal. But this time he had put on waterproofs and
was sorting out his pack in the mouth of the tent. I
wondered what was afoot.

'Getting ready for lift-off? A bit premature aren't we?'

'I want to find out what the problem is, why the *teniente*
isn't here. Just going to look at the river.'

He crawled out and slung on his rucksack. He did not
tell Peter and me that he was going to try and cross the
river to get to the French camp and fetch some food.

He plunged off into the driving rain and disappeared
down the berg. When he reached its lower edge he knew
why we had been left alone all day. The river which a week
ago had flowed clear and peaceful between the rounded
boulders in its bed was a red, raging flood.

Nick studied it for some time and then descended to the
point where it looked easiest to cross. He waded into the
river and the water swirled round his thighs. The force was
such that he was immediately bowled over and had difficulty
scrambling out. He picked another spot where the water
didn't seem to be running so fast but before he could get
very far out from the edge the torrent, beating against his
left hip, threatened to carry him downstream. There was no
way of getting a line made fast across the other side. The

French camp was a good half mile away and nobody was around in this evil weather. If he tried to struggle across whilst being slowly buffeted down-river he could perhaps have drowned in the process. If that happened, nobody would know; there would be no hope of being hauled out. And the thought was high in his mind, too, that there would be no succour for Peter and me.

He fought the river for a few more moments and then clambered out. Disconsolately he made his way back up the lava to the camp. As he climbed, he had the first premonitions of total disaster. It hadn't really occurred to any of us yet, but Nick now felt that we could all of us quite easily die if circumstances did not change in our favour. He had kept a brief diary going and now recalled some of the familiar phrases of Captain Scott's journal. Ought he perhaps to make some entry with posterity in mind? It may be a melodramatic notion but he could just be about to write one of the last pages. No, this was ridiculous; we had water enough, that was for sure, and even if our food and fuel *were* exhausted, well, he reasoned, those Irish hunger strikers in Portlaoise lasted for weeks before taking food. We would manage. But survival now might be a grim business.

Peter and I were silent when he returned. It wasn't always easy for us to chat because of Peter's acute stammer. So we had both slept while Nick was out. But awoken now, we sensed, and shared, his gloom.

He slowly explained the situation to us.

'I don't think we can expect the Special Forces chaps to risk one of their own lives to save ours,' was his verdict. 'They might just as well be a hundred miles away. That river cuts us right off from last night's helping hand.'

He got the stove going on its last few drops of fuel and prepared a hot drink. In doing so he found a bag of porridge oats in a rucksack pocket; they had been given to us by Ramón before he had left. It could make a lot of difference, we thought – and with reconstituted powdered milk began to seem, if not a gourmet's delight, at least palatable. We would hold it in reserve.

'Come on,' he urged, 'we mustn't sit like pigs in our own shit. Get mopping!' and he flung a face flannel into our tent with which Peter and I began to squeegee up some of the water around us. It was rather like bailing a leaky dinghy – we weren't certain whether the dripping from the tent walls was gaining on us.

It was some relief even to be doing this. Almost total inactivity saps the spirit and Peter and I were now virtually immobile. I had begun to fret at being such a burden to Nick, so incapable of the self-sufficiency that is normal on expeditions. At least we could make some personal efforts to prepare for the next ghastly night.

Considerable efforts on our behalf were being made at home, too. People in Britain were at this time languishing, not to say wilting, in the middle of the almost unbearably hot summer of '76. On the previous day Sergeant Mitcham had been Guard Commander at the Royal Military Academy, Sandhurst. Little had happened during the long, sultry Saturday afternoon, until, about 6 p.m. there was a phone message from the Duty Officer, Captain Rod Skidmore.

'Just had a call from the MOD,' he said. 'They want the next of kin name and address of a Mr Richard Snailham, one of the academics here. Could you try and trace them?'

This was a tough one and the sergeant's preliminary calls drew blanks. All the academic staff were on leave and those still at home seemed not to be indoors manning their telephones.

Time was slipping by when by a happy chance Sergeant Mitcham glanced down at the Academy Fishing Club book. This revealed that the key to the boathouse had been taken out by Dr Freddie Walker, Sandhurst's Deputy Director of Studies.

Mitcham left the guardroom, by the side of the Old Building, stately home of generations of potential army officers since 1812 and backdrop to numerous Sovereign's

Parades, jumped in his Land-Rover and drove through the parched grounds and down to the Lower Lake. A boat was anchored about a hundred metres from the bank.

Freddie Walker had for some time been casting for trout but with no success. The water in the lake was low and the trout were sluggish. He watched the Land-Rover drive down to the boathouse and flash its headlights. Packing up his tackle he rowed slowly over.

'Excuse me, sir, do you know the next of kin of Mr Snailham?'

'No, I don't think I do. Why?'

'There's been an accident in Ecuador, and the Ministry want to get in touch with them.'

Freddie feared the worst and sadly considered what to do. The Headquarters building, which probably contained the required information, was locked up. It would be a question of trying to find some close friend who might know.

'Leave it with me,' said Freddie. 'I'll go home now and ring you back.'

There then followed a chain of enquiries which, against all the odds, produced the results. Freddie phoned David Lewis, a colleague of mine in the same department. No, he didn't know, but would try Roy Leyland. Lieutenant-Colonel Roy Leyland, an ex-colleague, now retired, couldn't be sure, but thought it might be my mother. He telephoned Freddie Staples, my former landlord in Yateley. 'I think she lives in Sheffield, but Mrs Batt will know.' He phoned Mrs Edith Batt, a friend of my mother's, who was able to give name, address and phone number. So, through the good offices of five subscribers, all happily within earshot of their telephones, the information was relayed to Sergeant Mitcham and thence to Captain Skidmore and to the Ministry of Defence.

Just after midnight another request came, this time for my blood group. The sergeant found this out from the RMA Sandhurst Hospital and early on Sunday morning 'Blood group O Positive repeat O Positive' was signalled to the British defence attaché, Quito. On Saturday afternoon

(Quito time) Peter Wills had urgently sought information on all our blood groups and within six hours he had received it.

In the early hours of Sunday morning he set off from Quito to Riobamba and reached the military camp in pouring rain at 9 a.m. As ill chance would have it our own tragedy was followed by another, much graver, accident in Ecuador which had occurred that same morning. A Vickers Viscount of the local SAETA company with fifty-nine passengers on board disappeared on a domestic flight between Quito and the southern town of Cuenca. So just when Peter Wills hoped to be able to marshal the maximum Ecuadorean help towards our rescue there came this disaster, much nearer to the hearts of Ecuadoreans than our fate could ever be. Captain Agila's Alouette might well be diverted, with other FAE and army helicopters, and deployed over the miles of empty Andes in which the plane might have crashed.

Members of the Riobamba Andinista Club were assembling at the camp and Peter thought when he saw them that they might be headed for Sangay, but they were to spend the next days searching fruitlessly for the Viscount on the slopes of Chimborazo.

Our recovery was still given high priority, however, and a ground rescue team, including a doctor with supplies of blood of the right groups, was got together in case the weather continued to be bad. A British representative of Racal, currently in Quito in the hope of selling radio equipment to the Ecuadorean army, was driven down to Riobamba with a high frequency man-portable set for the ground rescue team.

The team, with doctor and radio, drove off towards the Hacienda Guarguallá in the late afternoon. Rain was bucketing down, the mud road was like a greasy pole and just short of Licto they passed a country bus which had rolled off it. A little further on they met a Land-Rover coming out. It contained Jeff Aucott and Bernardo Baete. The two men had spent an unpleasant and not very productive twenty-four hours at the hacienda. They had parked and slept under the tall eucalyptuses, as we had done, and on Sunday morning it was wet and misty. Cloud had filled the valley, obscuring the thatched cabins of the *peones* on the farther side of the Río Guarguallá. They had found a suitable helipad and marked it with orange tarpaulin. Jeff had the forty-five gallons of fuel with him, and his plan was for the helicopter to use the hacienda as a forward base. If the valleys from Riobamba to Guarguallá were blanketed in fog, the Alouette might nevertheless be able to slip over the *cordillera oriental* to Sangay and bring the wounded out to the hacienda.

But it had rained heavily all day and only in the late afternoon did a watery sun percolate through to dapple the wet mud in front of Fausto Merino's house for about five minutes. It had been enough of a break, however, to allow Captain Agila to take off. With Gerardo as guide he flew up to Guarguallá, circled the hacienda a couple of times and then, deciding it was still too bad, returned to Riobamba. Visibility must have become marginally better, for ten minutes later they took off again. Jeff and Bernardo ran from the hacienda to see the Alouette, at about 6.10 p.m., pass high above them and on up the river valley towards Sangay.

This was hopeful indeed. But Bolívar Agila knew well enough that it would very shortly grow dark and so, within ten minutes, he flew back once again over the hacienda to Riobamba. Light had long disappeared when he landed – just in time to attend a meeting of all the Viscount search team pilots held by the base commander, Colonel Raul Perez. It had been a brave effort, in atrocious conditions.

After a scratch supper Jeff, Bernardo and the Merino family were next called out to meet a string of mules with three *arrieros*. This was the French expedition's supply train, now returning.

A frustrating but vital interrogation followed: the three muleteers were closely questioned by Jeff about our condition, the Indians knowing none of our names and having to make do with descriptions of six Britons of whom Jeff had met only four. It was in this way that a crucial error was made. It was confirmed that Cooke was safe, and that Chadwick and I were safe but injured. It was conjectured, but with some certainty, that Ashby-Smith and Iwandziuk were the two dead and Mace the survivor with the severe head fracture.

Having established this as well as he could Jeff determined to drive straight away to Riobamba with the news. Thus it was that on his way in he met the ground rescue team coming out, and paused only to give the doctor some warning of the head injuries. And thus it was that Peter Wills telephoned his embassy on Monday with the text of a signal part of which read: 'two British (believed to be Iwandziuk and Ashby-Smith) were dead when found and a third (believed to be Ronald Mace) was unconscious with serious head injuries'.

Jan Iwandziuk's wife, Sarah, was at their new house in Whitfield, on the flat, Kentish hilltops behind Dover. Gerardo's first news had reached Britain on Saturday, 14 August, and the Royal Engineers Junior Leaders Regiment in Dover, where Jan was a troop commander, received it about the same time as Captain Skidmore had at Sandhurst. There was no difficulty in tracing Jan's next of kin. Lieutenant-Colonel John Blashford-Snell commanded the regiment and he personally came to break the news to Sarah.

It was still all very vague. Jan and his team had been caught up in a volcanic eruption, but inevitably Sarah suspected the worst and imagined herself a widow after only six months of marriage.

On the day of the eruption she had gone to one of John Blashford-Snell's famous parties at the officers' mess. It was in the form of a Graeco-Roman orgy. He had given one once before with this theme at his house near Swindon in 1967. There had been chariot-racing, jousting (John always has jousting whatever the historical period), and a great many vestal virgins were chased in and out of the bosky arbours which surrounded John's house. I had gone as Diogenes and wore a small barrel suspended from a pair of braces. It was an original dress but inhibited me greatly during the frenetic dancing which followed.

At Dover on 12 August the mess floor was strewn with pillows and mattresses. The officers wore togas or Roman armour and the tables groaned with joints of beef and roast chickens. A fountain was rigged up from which wine flowed. And once again there was chariot-racing. But as the evening wore on Sarah felt strangely unhappy and she left early.

Two days later the blow fell: Peter Chadwick and I were reported safe but the rest were 'missing'. So Sarah was for two days pitched into a limbo of uncertainty. As she was agonizing over Jan's fate more concrete news came through. But it can only have worsened her misery: two of the missing were now known to be dead. The erroneous belief that Jan was one of them was to cause much confusion at the Ministry of Defence but mercifully – and perhaps because of the note of doubt in Peter Wills's signal of Monday night – Sarah was not told of it.

In fact it was on the following day that she heard that he had been 'found' and was alive, though critically ill. This was a straw to clutch at, and she immediately began to make plans to get out to Ecuador.

At this point her husband, hanging precariously on to life, was still at the foot of Sangay. But he was no longer in our original base camp. The evening before, on Sunday, 15 August, we had lain damply in our tents and were at our most dejected. Communication between the three conscious survivors was almost nil. We had not eaten all day. Nick

Cooke was curled on the floor of his tent in great discomfort, waiting for his body warmth to dry the river water from his clothes. He had mopped the groundsheet again, changed Jan's trousers and sleeping bag and moved him so that the over-active left arm was out of range. But was the thrum of rain on our tent wall a little less insistent? I hardly dared to suggest it to Peter Chadwick. Perhaps, although it was late afternoon, there was a fraction more light?

I was roused from my torpor by the noise of a commotion outside. The flaps of the tent were torn back by an unseen figure and the whole camp seemed to be buzzing with activity.

'Come on!' shouted Nick. 'We're going!'

The Ecuadoreans, taking advantage of the slight lull in the rain, had found that the river level had dropped somewhat and had come *en masse* to fetch us to the French camp. My eyes were moistened with the emotion of the moment: we were no longer cut off from rescue by malevolent nature and doomed to sit out our last hours in isolation. We were to join the French – whose presence we had once so chauvinistically resented. There was a catch in our voices as Peter and I congratulated ourselves on our good luck.

'Never mind your kit. They'll pack it up,' Nick added. 'Just get out of your tent and they'll take you down.'

Painfully Peter and I struggled into our boots. Even standing up was quite a performance. All around us swarthy little soldiers were stuffing equipment and clothing into rucksacks and dismantling the tents. A litter had been constructed and under Didio Romero's guidance they were slowly manoeuvring Jan onto it. In the light evening rain Nick supervised the operation whilst packing his own kit.

I soon found that I could scarcely walk. But it did not matter: with Cabo II Fausto Racines on one arm and Cabo I Segundo Lucero slightly more gingerly on the other I was soon being carefully manhandled down the berg.

Peter hobbled ahead of me, similarly chaperoned, and past us all strode other soldiers loaded up with our gear.

Jan, watched by Nick and his devoted *enfermero*, came along behind.

The river was still an obstacle. But six legs are better than two, and clasped firmly together we managed to force it. I found that the most painful movement for me was an upwards step and so when we reached the far side my two supporters had to grasp each other's crossed hands and chair me up the bank.

'Is it very far?' I kept asking feebly.

'It is near here,' they reassured me, *'es cerca de aquí. Cien metros.'*

But it was an excruciatingly long drag, and every hundred metres seemed to be followed by another.

Finally we reached the big lava berg we had crossed on the way in. I laboured up it and on its flat top, the size of a football pitch, stood the dull green tents of the Ecuadorean army and the bright orange and blue ones of the French. Porters, soldiers and scientists stood about in groups and watched us coming in: there must have been upwards of fifty people in the camp. My eyes filled again as I tottered gratefully into their midst.

10

Espoir et Désespoir

Fortune is painted blind, with a muffler afore her eyes, to signify to you that Fortune is blind; and she is painted also with a wheel, to signify to you, which is the moral of it, that she is turning, and inconstant, and mutability, and variation; and her foot, look you, is fixed upon a spherical stone, which rolls, and rolls, and rolls.

Henry V, III, vi, 30–6

It must be a rare thing in life for men to go from such grim despair to such unsurpassed elation in as swift a way as we did. Our arrival in the French camp was certainly one of the most moving moments I can recall. We were not yet by any means home and dry, but life certainly had taken on a rosy glow with amazing suddenness. As Nick afterwards put it: 'Although we weren't noticeably better off, because we'd come back into the community of other men who were living and strong and vigorous and welcoming and loving, we felt ourselves immeasurably richer and more secure.'

Teniente Palacios told his men to make room for us in one of their two big bell tents and this they cheerfully did. They were already grossly overcrowded and soldiers were lying side by side on the canvas floor like the segments of half an orange. However, they shuffled apart and Nick, Peter and I lay stiffly down among them all.

Haroun Tazieff's eight scientists called in in ones and twos to meet us, and unfailingly they asked what they might bring us. Our own kit was being unpacked outside and soon a dry sleeping bag appeared, some dry trousers, a sweater, a duvet and a clean pair of long, thick stockings for each of us. What we had brought from our base camp was wholly wet and unwearable, so in most cases this clean clothing belonged to the French – which was some sacrifice as it was chill and dank still, and they had travelled very lightly from Guarguallá in order to reach us as fast as possible. The US Army pattern sleeping bags came from the Ecuadoreans and looked as if they would give magnificent all-round warmth.

At the entrance to the tent was a large cauldron filled with vermicelli soup. As we settled in, a mug of this was brought to each of us. It was not very palatable and Nick had to ask for salt, but we soon had internal as well as external heating.

'Hey, d-did you see the woman?' Peter asked me.

'A woman. What's that?'

'The w-woman. There's a woman in Tazieff's team.'

'Yes, I saw her,' said Nick. 'She's good news.'

This was an unexpected fillip to our fortunes, and I was not to be disappointed when a young girl, fine-featured and with short, black hair, came into our tent. Isabelle Garma was an Argentinian from Paris, spoke French and Spanish fluently, and was with Tazieff as an interpreter, to handle his expedition's administrative liaison with the Ecuadoreans. Sensibly dressed in thick blue sweater and trousers, she seemed in no way out of place in such aggressively male company.

She was nevertheless an astonishing person to encounter in this wilderness and proved to be important to us at all sorts of levels. At the most basic, it was marvellous to come across someone with a bumpy chest; then we found it a very considerable comfort to be able to talk to someone who had all the sympathy, warmth and considerateness of her sex; furthermore, she spoke good English, and this was a boon to Peter and Nick for whom there were linguistic barriers in a Franco-Ecuadorean gathering.

Haroun Tazieff, who presently came in to greet us, can have experienced few of these language problems in his

extensive wanderings about the world in search of volcanoes. He speaks French, Spanish, Russian, English,
Arabic and no doubt a great many more tongues, with a
facility and charm that must everywhere endear him to his
audience. A small, gnome-like figure, in immaculately
fashionable French climbing gear – boots, long stockings,
breeches and anorak, topped off with a blue woollen hat
with a white pompom – he was deeply interested in our
adventures and spent much of the evening crouched among
the Ecuadorean soldiers chatting to Nick and me. Sixty-four
and sandy-grey now, with a gnarled, weather-beaten face,
he radiated a genuine friendliness and concern that was in
itself a morale-booster. We all loved him immediately – and
thought how absurd it was that we had first considered him
as some sort of unsporting, Gallic intruder into our territory.

We were now in many respects his responsibility, though
we were all of us also the responsibility of Teniente Palacios,
who bustled in and out with an air of great efficiency and
authority. Between them they had decided to place Jan in
one of the scientists' two-man tents, while they had had
Adrian's body in its sleeping bag laid on the flat berg a
little distance away from the camp. Cabo II Didio Romero
had instantly gone to work on Jan, cleaning him, warming
him and feeding him. And Jan had continued to respond
to this treatment and to make encouraging noises.

As darkness fell the soldiers congregated in the tent and
drew across the canvas entrance flap to exclude some of the
night cold. They were a hardy lot – little men with stubby
fingers, uniformly black hair militarily cropped and high
cheekbones like seasoned conkers. They joked and chaffed
and fought each other playfully as if they were so many
labrador pups.

When they had settled down somewhat a cry went up for
'François!' and within a moment or two, and to great
acclamation, François Le Guern appeared. He was one
of Tazieff's volcanologists, but the instrument he was to use
tonight was more rhythmic than seismic. He wormed his

way into our midst, pulled a mouth-organ from his top pocket and began to play a series of haunting Breton melodies. He had obviously established his reputation on the preceding evenings and to shouts of '*Más! Más!*' one song succeeded another. More Frenchmen appeared, then Isabelle and Haroun again, and the mouth-organ gave way to voice.

First we had a French song, than an Ecuadorean, but all joined in where they could. Even the three of us were able to add volume to some of the choruses.

As François played I lay back and thought of the many holidays I had spent driving through the Midi on *voies départementales* with the car radio playing those catchy accordion pieces that pour incessantly from French provincial stations. All over Europe – in Borrowdale, at Azay-le-Rideau, by Lake Constance – groups of young people were even now gathered together round camp fires or in tents as we were, clapping hands and singing national songs. It still seemed beyond belief that I should be doing the same under a live volcano in the remote Andes.

After some while there was a convenient lull. I had been wondering for a time whether the moment had come for something English. I explained briefly that mine was a regional English song, famous but perhaps difficult for foreigners to fathom. It was about a man who went with his girlfriend onto a moor '*sans chapeau – sin sombrero*'. He caught a cold and died and so his friends had to – well, it was complicated, but it wouldn't matter if they didn't understand it because my two southern colleagues probably wouldn't either.

'Wheer 'astha bin sin ah saw thee . . .' I began rather quaveringly.

It seemed to go down quite well – and the therapeutic effect it had on me was considerable.

When the sing-song was over more Ecuadoreans piled into the tent and a second stratum of bodies began to overlay the first. It looked like a student bid for the bell-tent capacity record. I found a rather damp, squashed cigar and smoked it, as soldiers undressed and bedded down all round. Soon I burrowed like a hamster into my down-filled bag, arranged my right arm in its most comfortable position – straight along my side, swallowed some antibiotics and fell asleep.

Monday morning was bleak and bitter. Through the door I saw the rain weeping down. It had been a restless night for us all and few had slept much. The cold had struck up through the canvas floor and penetrated our cocoons. I had twisted and shifted to try to achieve a tolerable lie and at every contortion my bones had chafed painfully together like a fenderless boat at a quayside.

'*Buenos días*, Marco,' I said to my right-hand neighbour, an engineer from the Survey Department, as I slowly jacked myself up on my left elbow.

In a little while the cheerful, rounded face of Cabo II Fausto Racines, who had helped to carry me down the previous day, loomed over us with a tin mug in each hand.

'*Carne!*' he said, beaming.

Gobbets of grey meat floated in a thin gruel. He pointed outside to where the shaggy skin of a wild deer was already strung up to dry. It was an unorthodox breakfast, but nourishing.

Waiting is always wearisome, and few people stirred from their sleeping bags. There was nothing that I could do except talk. Isabelle came to us during the morning and, like a good occupational therapist, chatted about her work and travels. Haroun also came and told us of his exploits at Nyiragongo, Irazu and Etna.

He told us, too, of his interests in Sangay, and they seemed to coincide materially with Peter Francis's. We pooled our knowledge of the mountain: he explained what he knew of its volcanic performance, and I outlined the history of previous sightings and ascents.

We talked of the 1628 eruption, of Charles Marie de la Condamine's account of an eruption of 1739 that appeared 'to set on fire the whole mountain and its crater', while a 'burning river of sulphur and bitumen took its course in the midst of the snowy slopes'; of a geologist called Reiss who told of incandescent lava flowing from Sangay's western shoulder for four years without a break; of an engineer called Wisse who counted 267 eruptions in the course of an hour. We discussed Commander Dyott's brave attempt of 1925 in which, after many setbacks, he reached about 16800 feet on his first ascent. His porters had been wading about in the deep snow with bare feet and nearly deserted, but with his London companion, G. C. Johnston, he climbed again until the exhaustion of floundering in snow drifts checked them at just over 17000 feet. 'We waited a week for favourable weather, which failed to materialize' was a comment of Dyott's which now came back to my mind.*

I carried with us in my rucksack, carefully folded in polythene envelopes, photocopies of accounts of some of the twentieth-century ascents and so we were able to check our experiences against those of Dyott, Moore, Lewis, Bonington and Snow.

'Who first actually gained the summit?' asked Haroun.

'An American zoologist, Robert T. Moore, in 1929,' I said. 'And he seems to have had the same problem that we all had in getting down off the thing. Look at this bit: "So impenetrable are the jungles of the steep eastern slope that no one has attacked the summit from this direction" – this was written before Bonington and Snow went, of course. "On the other three sides, 1000 square miles of volcanic ash have been sculpted by almost constant rains into a labyrinth of black canyons 500 to 2000 feet deep. Down each one swirls an angry torrent – the whole constituting a veritable maze, whose intricacies have never been deeply penetrated . . ." Well, in spite of mutinous porters and twenty-six days of continuous rain four of them crossed this labyrinth and put up an advanced camp at 16000 feet. They were lashed by a violent hailstorm during the night, and next day the steepness of the ice-covered slopes and their lack of an

* *The Volcanoes of Ecuador, Guideposts in Crossing South America*, G. M. Dyott (National Geographic Magazine, Vol. LV, No. 1, Jan. 1929).

ice-axe defeated them. The day after that they climbed again
and reached the highest point on the rim of an 800-foot-long
crater about mid-day. They spent three hours at the summit
taking pictures! And, you know, what I can't get over is
this – those four Americans were at a height of 16000 feet
or above – the height we were knocked off at – for fifty-one
hours!'

'Well, someone has to get the bad luck,' said Haroun.
'But I'm truly sorry it was you.'

'See what it says here: "It did not give us concern, since
an eruption is generally preceded by seismic disturbances of
a violent nature . . .". That certainly didn't happen with us.'

'It often doesn't in a Strombolian type of eruption,'
Haroun explained.

'Have there been any recent expedition ascents?' asked
Isabelle.

'Yes. Two Ecuadoreans, Celso Zuquillo and Marco Cruz,
made a trip here in 1972,' I said, 'but I don't know much
about it. The next big party came from the Escuela Politécnica Nacional and was led by Dr Minard Hall in the
summer of 1975. Ten men with two guides and four porters
came in from Alao – part of the way with mules – by the
"old" Río Culebrillas route, across Moore's "labyrinth" in
fact, and camped somewhere near here. On their fifth day
out they climbed Sangay. Twice on the way up the whole
sky suddenly darkened and seconds afterwards they felt ash
falling on them. The ground was like a chocolate cream
layer cake, with successive strata of snow and ash. After the
second ash fall their guides turned and ran down the
mountain, calling back "*Feliz viaje!*" as they disappeared
into the fog!'

'You can hardly blame the b-buggers!' chipped in Peter
Chadwick.

'Three other climbers followed them, but the rest pushed
on. We know all this because the guy who hired us the ropes
and crampons and the ice-axes, Allan Miller of the Forestry
Department, was one of them.'

'We'll have to do a bit of reckoning up with him when

we get back,' said Nick, 'because I feel certain we've lost half that stuff.'

'Go on. What happened to them?' said Isabelle.

'Nothing really. They got to the top but there was such a lot of sulphur dioxide swirling about that they came down after a few minutes.'

'What sort of gear did they use?' Haroun asked.

'They had crampons, but they didn't use helmets or ropes.'

'So the volcano was pretty quiet for them, too?'

'Yes. Apparently at the *choza** by the Culebrillas on the way in the weather lifted for a moment one evening and they saw red-hot lava spilling down the north-west face of the cone. But that seems to have been all – throughout six days and nights.'

'Any other ascents?'

'Some time earlier this year Minard Hall, who's president of the International Andean Mountaineers in Quito, went with a World Wildlife Fund expedition to this area. They weren't really a mountaineering team but they did attempt a climb. There was too much activity, though, and they had to retreat and spent three days in their tents, penned in by incessant rain.'

'Which seems to have been the story on every expedition.'

'Listen to it now,' said Nick.

'Minard Hall seems to have a Sangay fixation,' I added. 'His visit of last week was at least his third. And he's going to fly over it to get some aerials.'

'It's a mountain I could easily give up,' said Nick.

News of a very disturbing kind then arrived to break into our discussion. One of the French scientists had a transistor, and he had heard a news bulletin announcing the crash of the SAETA Viscount. Helicopters and aircraft of the Ecuadorean air force, together with teams of local *andinistas*, were being mobilized at Riobamba to carry out the search for the missing plane. We realized immediately

* *choza* = grass hut.

that this would materially affect our chances of rescue. It would probably mean a party of expatriate Brits laboriously coming out overland to pick us up.

Our dismay at this news was not entirely justified. Captain Bolívar Agila and his Alouette were still at our disposal and during that wet Monday morning – which was, most unusually, wet in Riobamba, too – the cloud lifted enough to permit him to fly again to Guarguallá. There he picked up a French member of Tazieff's team who had been left to operate our Racal HF radio set but who had had communication problems. When they got back to Riobamba, new frequencies were chosen and the Frenchman was returned to Guarguallá, where Captain Agila waited in the hopes of a mid-day lift in the cloud level. But there was no change, so at 2 p.m. he was back at the military base.

Two other Alouettes had, however, arrived at Riobamba and were dipping into the fuel supply that we had had brought down from Quito: as Peter Wills wrote in his Tuesday signal home, 'It has become every man for himself.' So a further irony could be that the petrol might run out just as the weather improved.

Peter Wills and Jeff Aucott, together now, were being harassed by press and television men who were hanging around the military base, with several hundred relatives and friends of the missing passengers. The three-man overland rescue team had flown back there that afternoon in the Alouette, having been unable to cross the first big river beyond Guarguallá.

Later in the day Captain Agila flew out to the hacienda again – his sixth sortie – to await a possible weather improvement. It did clear a little eventually and the helicopter took a consignment of food for Tazieff's expedition to the halfway point at Plaza Pamba, and was able to get a good way towards Sangay before being driven back by thick cloud. Agila had no radio contact with Riobamba, and there was great concern at the base when, an hour after sunset, he had still not returned. However, he had been using his last few drops of fuel to search for the lost Viscount on the slopes of Chimborazo, still illuminated by the setting sun.

Colonel Perez had assured a sceptical Peter Wills that a 2000-gallon tanker was expected to arrive that day with more fuel. Nothing came. Our situation was set out with stark simplicity by Peter in one of his signals:

A. There are two confirmed fatalities and probably a third.

B. The only possible method of casevac for remainder (who have multiple injuries) is by heli.

C. Sangay base is above 12000 feet and has not cleared since heli became available.

D. Organized renewable fuel supply has not been set up. . . .

E. Casevac could be effected quickly if weather clears, but it is equally possible that there could be delay of week or more.

This possibility occurred to me as I lay clutching my right arm, now filled with infection and swollen to a banana shape. During a dry spell I stood up and with difficulty staggered out into the crisp air. Humming-birds darted about and the occasional brown hawk soared overhead as I walked to the edge of the berg for a pee.

Our camp was like a small village. Groups of people strolled up and down on the lava – the evening *paseo* in the plaza of any Spanish town. I came back to Jan's tent. Nick had suggested that I should try and get through to him. He had not yet opened his eyes but Corporal Romero had succeeded in feeding him some soup and perhaps if he recognized my voice he would respond to it.

He lay on his back wrapped in a silver foil space blanket, still and waxen like the marble effigy of a dead Medici.

'Hello, Jan,' I said. 'It's Richard.'

There was a long moment of stillness before his mouth slowly opened.

'Hello, Richard,' said a childlike voice.

A wonderful, hopeful moment. I told him in simple terms that all was well and that we would soon be rescued.

'We're with the French,' I added. 'They're looking after us all.'

'Hello, Richard,' Jan replied.

A crowd of soldiers, porters and guides were milling about round a cauldron. The big bulk of Sergeant Cadena stood behind it dishing out lunch. Fausto Racines came up to me and said '*Comida?*' with a lift of his eyebrows.

'*Sí, por favor,*' I said, and he soon reappeared with a piece of burnt meat on a skewer. It was burnt rather than roasted, and very fatty. I could make little of it. That afternoon the carcasses of two more grey deer were brought in on poles and I blenched at the prospect of being marooned here for several days on an unending diet of ill-prepared venison. The Ecuadorean army seemed not to give its people any set rations, and the *teniente* was expected somehow to feed his twenty men by foraging and hunting.

It was a hard country to live off, and this corner of it particularly so. I longed for the composite, varied British army rations – little packets to unwrap, little tins to open, a choice of different menus, a mixture of savoury and sweet, bland and piquant – though my present situation perhaps lent them an added enchantment. I refused a second helping of *carne* and stood talking to some of the French scientists.

Sangay, intermittently visible, loomed over us all, still but menacing. Its white mantle now stretched the whole way down its flanks, for the previous night it had snowed heavily. Patches of white dappled the *paja* grass on the hillside behind our encampment. Haroun Tazieff strode about, occasionally filming scenes of camp life with an expensive Japanese cine-camera. He had an awkward decision to make – should he persist in his survey of Sangay? Our arrival in his midst had affected his plans greatly, but if we were picked up soon surely his eight scientists could go ahead and do something useful, after all the expenses of time and money and the marshalling of this large army in support? The grim tale of our disaster had its effect on him, too, and the continuing unpropitious weather, the difficulty of getting his stores from Guarguallá, the recent heavy fall of soft snow, all combined to make him decide to retreat from the mountain.

But he had first to await our rescue and as cloud came down low over the ridges to the west of us and rain fell again, things did not look too hopeful. Teniente Palacios, a powerful figure in his black poncho, was superintending the skinning and evisceration of the two grey deer. He had his decisions to make, too. His men were chafing. Idleness was bad for them. The weather in this part of the eastern cordillera was notorious – it may be weeks before it broke up sufficiently to let a helicopter in to Sangay. Camp must be struck and the move back to Guarguallá begun. At first light tomorrow morning we would march!

There was widespread consternation in mid-afternoon when the news of this decision broke. It was mainly in the hearts of Nick, Peter and me – particularly me. But the French felt it vicariously. I could not imagine how I should endure a punishing, three- or maybe four-day march up and down near-vertical lava ridges, along precipitous cols, through raging rivers, even with the promised support of two husky soldiers at either side. Peter had grave doubts, too, and even Nick seemed a bit cast down. The *teniente* proposed that his men should carry Jan on an improvised wooden litter, but I did not rate highly his chances of surviving such a protracted agony. First Haroun Tazieff discussed the question with the lieutenant, and then, to employ Latin-American charm where patient Gallic logic had failed, Isabelle was sent to urge him to delay the move for just a couple more days to give a helicopter some further chances. But he was obdurate. His mind was made up and we would leave at dawn on Tuesday.

My friend Fausto encouraged me to try out a few practice steps on the berg, and so in the late afternoon I stomped around the perimeter of the camp with him, lifting my knees in simulation of the climbing that now faced me. It was acutely painful: certain body movements jarred my upper arm but, worse than that, my left leg would barely lift as a result of the blow I had taken low down on my back.

'*Vamonos!*' he shouted, propelling me along, '*Arriba! Vamonos!*'

I stepped out unconvincingly as he gripped my good arm, clenched his left fist, and with a grimace of determination said, '*Fuerza moral! Fuerza moral!*'

My quota of moral courage seemed dismally small, but round and round I went, trying to recover the rhythms of marching once again.

As we proceeded jerkily along there was another grim reminder of the lieutenant's determination to move. Some of his men were digging a grave for Adrian out on the berg. It would be a back-breaking task to carry him to Guargualá and he could not just be left out in the open in his sleeping bag.

'Richard,' said Nick, 'I wonder if you would say a few words over his body when we bury him?'

'Sure,' I replied, and my mind began to race as I searched it for whatever parts of the Order for the Burial of the Dead that I could recall. . . . 'The Lord gave and the Lord hath taken away' . . . 'In the midst of life we are in death' . . . 'Earth to earth, ashes to ashes, dust to dust'. . . . But would Adrian want such church formulae as these? I expected that I should be able to string something together.

The actual moment was so charged with emotion that I have no memory of what I said. He was laid in the shallow grave, but the light was failing and the soldiers decided to wait until the next morning before throwing the spoil heap of lava over him.

As I crawled to my sleeping bag and clumsily began to take off boots and stockings I reflected on fate's cruelty to us so far. I had never known such a succession of blows followed by rays of hope followed by further blows: after the eruption Peter and I had had a chance of effecting a quick rescue but had been caught in the labyrinth of ravines, thus committing Nick to his terrible night on the mountain; he had then set off hopefully for help but had missed the guides on their way up; the French had arrived with an Ecuadorean medic, which raised our morale, but rains and wind had come to prevent us joining them and effectively cutting us off from all aid, which dashed it again. Now we had reached the French, to await whatever rescue Gerardo had been able to ˙arrange, and Teniente Palacios had resolved to set us off on a desparate march to Guarguallá.

'*Espoir et désespoir*,' I said to one of the scientists, 'I don't think I can take much more of it.'

II

Lark at Break of Day Arising

> Adrian's body was lying in a shallow open grave dug with
> ice-axes out of the black cinder mud. It was a beautiful and
> lonely spot . . . looking up at the smoking volcano which
> had killed him. I think he would have enjoyed lying there in
> the wilderness he loved so much.
>
> Nick Cooke, *Diary*

At 11.30 p.m. on Monday night Jeff Aucott again left
Riobamba in his Land-Rover with a forty-five-gallon drum
of fuel lashed down in the back (the promised tanker had,
in fact, arrived). He drove over the now familiar track to
Guarguallá, where he found Bernardo Baete with the
Merino family. The Alouette could once more use the
helipad at the hacienda as a base for mercy runs to Sangay.

At much the same time Peter Wills, who had left his
embassy office in something of a hurry, drove back from
Riobamba to Quito to collect some personal gear in readi-
ness for a long siege and to bring back the Racal engineer,
Mr A. Hewitt, to clear up the communications difficulties.
It was planned that the man-portable HF radio would be
taken to Guarguallá by Hewitt and a volunteer doctor, who
would, if need be, join Jeff Aucott and Bernardo Baete in
an overland march to Sangay. In this way were our rescuers
once more to be deployed.

It was a brilliant, starlit night when Jeff reached the
hacienda at 1 a.m. 'The moon was just beginning to come
up at this stage,' said Jeff afterwards, 'casting long shadows
from the eucalyptus trees onto the hillside and creating a

silvery, eerie glow.' There were no clouds and for once
conditions looked auspicious for the helicopter.

With no cloud cover it was, of course, colder than usual
and Jeff was cheered to see Bernardo produce a bottle of
whisky.

'Yes, I'll just have one with you, Bernardo,' Jeff said.

It took them about an hour to polish it all off. At this
stage Jeff realized that he had lent his sleeping bag to one
of the Frenchmen in Tazieff's team, so he wrapped himself
in his space blanket and curled up in the back of the Land-
Rover, hoping that it would trap some of the effects of the
whisky as they ebbed from his tired body.

At the Franco-Ecuadorean camp we also noticed that it
was a clear, starry night. Before we turned in we had
watched Sangay putting on a valedictory display for us. The
summit glowed as red-hot lava was disgorged over its
western lip.

On watch one night between Malta and the toe of Italy,
I had been encouraging the Sandhurst cadets with me to
keep their eyes skinned for the lights marking the Straits
of Messina. As often happens, we had fallen to examining
the night sky which was unparalleled in its clarity. 'What's
that, sir?' asked one of my watch, indicating a cigar-shaped
patch of red high above the horizon to the west. I had said,
rather carelessly, 'I expect it's the moon rising.'

'But we've already got one over there,' another cadet
pointed out helpfully. This was worrying. It was the sort of
material those UFO stories are often grounded on. It was
a moment or two before I realized that what we were
looking at, from some forty miles distance, was the incandescent summit of Etna.

Sangay was nearer to home, unmistakable and an awe-
inspiring backdrop against which to play out our last few
hours on the berg. The dreadful prospect of the next days'
march made me consciously relish these few hours of supine
inactivity, however uncomfortable. I knew how important
it was to rest fully and deeply, and perversely my keenness
to do so kept sleep at bay for a valuable hour or two.

At the other end of the night I had similar difficulties. My troubled mind seemed only tentatively to cross the threshold of sleep and it stepped back over it again into wakefulness at about 4 a.m. I lay and fretted that I would be in no shape at all for a day of maximum physical activity. The more I agonized over the problem the more crystal-sharp and alert my thoughts became. It seemed a very long time before Marco Jácome, on my right, and Teniente Palacios, on his right, stirred and woke. One or two soldiers were unzipping their bags when the tent door was snatched open and Sergeant Cadena rapped out a curt order.

It was still as black as the Styx outside. The torches of our soldiers bobbed about as they dressed. By their occasional light I one-handedly hauled on my boots and got Nick to tie them up. This was it, then. There was no stopping our inexorable departure. No final intercession from Isabelle was likely, nor would it have succeeded. The trial would surely begin. I wondered if I was the only one who felt it so keenly. Nick and Peter seemed to be taking things remarkably stoically. I had made no secret of my apprehension, but they had both kept pretty silent.

I rammed a few possessions into my rucksack – I appeared to have far fewer than when I had arrived. I had given Jan my thick blue sweater up on the mountain just after the eruption and so far as I knew he still wore it, my sodden sleeping bag was hanging, with the others, over a *choza*, ostensibly to dry, and one of the soldiers was running about in a peaked, khaki cap of curious pattern, which my secretary had given me. The sleeping bags, together with our petrol stove, were much coveted and bid for and it was now that Nick suddenly could not find his belt and water bottle. I felt it an almost insuperable task to centralize and account for everything. A disaster lowers one's defences, and it was in these moments of total dependence on others that we lost a lot of our kit.

The early light of dawn began to filter under the sides of the bell tent, which was now emptying as the soldiers set to work outside.

'Do my flies up, there's a good soul,' I said to Nick.

Peter was being similarly attended to by his two neighbours. I suppose that it is mathematically logical that dressing should take the one-armed just twice as long, but it seemed to be taking us three or four times as long.

A couple of days earlier, when we had been conveyed down the berg to join the French, our fortunes had swung from rock bottom to cloud nine. But the see-saw process itself took about an hour to complete and so its impact had been modified.

Now there occurred a similar reversal of fortune, a similar translation from abject gloom to unalloyed bliss. But this time it was instantaneous. From down the valley there stole upon our ears a magical sound – the unmistakable, rapid 'gully-gully-gully-gully-gully . . .' of an approaching helicopter.

Nick rushed outside and Peter's face was suddenly radiant as he flung up his arm in joy. Crouched over my rucksack I hung my head as tears filled my eyes. Relief, incredulity, thankfulness in equal measures suffused me. I was too slow-moving to get out and see the Alouette touch down but carried on packing as hastily as I could.

Nick in his joy had just kissed Christophe, one of the Frenchmen – a strange reversal of national customs. Now he ran back into the tent.

'Quick as you can, Richard. Jan, you and Peter first. He won't want to hang around. These chaps never do.'

As I emerged I saw the helicopter silhouetted against a perfect sky. The rotor blades were still turning smartly and the pilot, the pertinacious Captain Bolívar Agila, remained in his seat. There were a few hurried good-byes and Peter and I ran forward with our rucksacks, tucking in our shirt-tails as we went and ducking instinctively as the downdraught struck us.

Jan had already been lifted on board in his sleeping bag, but the body of the Alouette was not broad enough to permit him to lie at full length. His head and shoulders were awkwardly propped up against the far door. I climbed in to

rearrange him slightly and found myself wedged in at the
end, unable to stand fully upright. But this way I could
keep an eye on his head. Peter took a seat next to the co-
pilot, Teniente Carrasco, rucksacks were flung in the back,
and with no further ado Captain Agila throttled up and we
lifted slowly above the camp.

Hovering for a second or two over the sea of upturned
faces we returned the salutes of Nick, Haroun, Isabelle and
their friends, of the soldiers, guides and porters, before
pulling away and executing the helicopter's characteristic,
dragonfly swoop down the length of the berg.

We climbed fast and soon the deep *quebradas* of Moore's
'labyrinth' were below us, row after row of ridges, a
foaming torrent in the valley between each. The grassy
folds of the eastern cordillera lay ahead.

Journeys by helicopter are in my experience uniquely
breathtaking in the suddenness and the completeness of the
transition they provide, more so even than transitions by
winged aircraft which generally have flown me between
sophisticated airports with all their intervening barriers,
departure lounges, duty-free zones and customs halls. All
the delays and *longueurs* of ordinary air travel – finding the
airport, checking in, waiting for the flight call, trudging
down those endless tunnels only to wait again, settling into
the plane, taxi-ing to the take-off point . . . and the same in
reverse at the other end – are dispensed with. One minute
I have been lying in a dark German pinewood with my hair
full of leaves, and the next been whisked over the north
German plain, to be sipping coffee twenty minutes later on
the open-air verandah at Düsseldorf airport. Or, more
dramatically, I have walked in climbing gear down from
Idwal Slabs towards the Ogwen valley at 2 p.m., been lifted
in a Sioux over Snowdonia and, with a pause at Birming-
ham for fuel, on over England's broad shires to be deposited
at Sandhurst two hundred yards outside the officers' mess
just before the steward brought in the tea. The disorienta-
tion is terrific.

Now we thrummed steadily over the desolate land, ahead

of us always the snowy mass of Chimborazo. The rising sun picked out its glorious 20560-foot-high cone in sharp relief, climbed first by Whymper almost a century before. I envied Peter Chadwick his dress circle seat, for the painfulness of my stance made it difficult to enjoy the superb view. Of all the helicopter flights I have made this was beyond doubt the most scenically ravishing. Yet it seemed wrong somehow to take pleasure in it at all, and every now and then a glance down at Jan's broken head put things in perspective for me. It was no joyride. We had to get him to hospital fast, to try and save his life.

For forty-five minutes Chimborazo and the dusty little town of Riobamba drew slowly nearer. Tiny fields appeared now below us, and farmsteads and tracks. We would soon be decanted into a bustling throng of FAE ground staff, medical orderlies, reporters and photographers. Captain Agila and his co-pilot performed their vital, life-saving role in professional silence. None of us exchanged a single word in the entire flight. It was as well, because I was beginning to feel emotionally very mixed up.

The last few miles seemed interminable, but soon we identified the military base of the *Brigada Blindada 'Galápagos' No. 1* and circled down into it. The door was wrenched open and a knot of anxious brown faces confronted us. First of all Jan was carried carefully into an ambulance, then Peter and I were helped out and, after thanking the pilots (without realizing then that it was seventh time lucky for them after an exhausting three days), we walked across the tarmac to a waiting minibus, preceded by cameramen and journalists from *El Comercio*, *El Tiempo* and sundry radio stations. There was nobody there whom we recognized, which we thought a little odd.

Peter Wills, who had done so much to set up the machinery of rescue, missed this supreme moment. Ironically, on his way back from Quito, the accelerator cable on his embassy car had snapped and his anguished driver had spent precious minutes effecting a temporary repair. They did not reach Riobamba until we were all in hospital there.

At the moment we touched down Jeff Aucott, with
Bernardo Baete, was out at Guarguallá. At six o'clock he
had risen to a perfect morning and seen the Alouette
passing up the valley at high altitude. There was a fair
amount of aerial activity all round at that time for this was
also the first good day for the search for the missing
SAETA airliner. But among the various planes and helicopters buzzing about there was one that was quite un-
connected with either rescue attempt and indeed oblivious
of them. Minard Hall, the American *profesor principal* of
geology at the Polytechnic, had hired a plane to take his
long-desired air photographs of Sangay. On this same
brilliant morning he circled the volcano and flew close over
its three craters to get a unique portfolio of excellent
pictures, some of which appear by his permission in this
book.

After dropping Peter Chadwick, Jan and me Captain
Agila set off immediately on his eighth run towards Sangay.
This time he had with him two *andinistas* and when they
reached the Franco-Ecuadorean camp Nick pointed out as
well as he could the place on the volcano's flank where Ron
Mace's body lay. The Alouette picked up Hector Vásquez,
an Ecuadorean climber, and Sergeant Cadena and flew
away over the river, past the site of our base camp and up
towards the summit. But the heavy snowfall of Sunday
night and Monday morning had obliterated everything.
There was no sign of Ron, nor was Captain Agila able to be
sure that he was in exactly the right area. Although the
rescuers had an altimeter and climbing rope they were
otherwise ill-equipped, with no crampons or stretcher.
Sangay began to vomit smoke and things looked pretty
ominous, so the pilot gave up the search and returned to
deposit his mountaineers at the French camp.

Adrian's body was then lifted aboard, much of our
remaining gear was unceremoniously bundled in on top of
him and Nick took the seat between pilot and co-pilot.
Flying back, he shared my simple sensation of amazement
that we should so easily be whisked over the forbidding,

Visibility always worsened during the day, so Nick tapped in
marker flags for our return

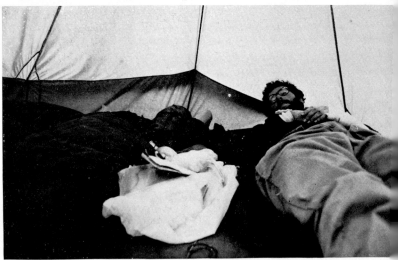

After the disaster we nevertheless lost our way down confusingly similar couloirs

With shattered right arms the author and Peter Chadwick await rescue in their tent

Gerardo greets the author and Peter at Riobamba after their helicopter flight from Sangay

An information centre was set up at Dover by John Blashford-Snell. During his appearance in Thames Television's 'This is Your Life' I told a story from our Blue Nile adventures

Nick Cooke and his George Medal outside Buckingham Palace

empty territory that we had so laboriously toiled over on foot. He saw the Merino haciendas at Guargualla and Alao with their lines of eucalyptus trees, and landed at Riobamba amidst an even larger throng of curious bystanders. He sensed a natural disappointment among them that he was not an Ecuadorean from the crashed Viscount, but there was nevertheless great concern and interest at the arrival of one who had survived an eruption of *El majestuoso Sangay* – with the corpse of one who had not.

A single familiar figure forced a way to the front. Gerardo Herrera, caught unawares by the previous arrival of the Alouette, now came forward, half anxious, half relieved, to clasp Nick in a bear-hug. None of us knew yet the details of the part Gerardo had played in our recovery but Nick, who had not seen him since before the eruption, expressed all our gratitude before being driven off through a sea of photographers and reporters to hospital.

There, in the tender hands of a Mother Superior and her nursing sisters, he had his head cleaned and anointed and his leg injury attended to and then, still in his long orange cagoul and soaking wet trousers, he sat out in the hot sun to dry off. The sisters then produced a perfect welcome – a boiled egg, coffee and rolls – his first regular breakfast for two weeks.

Jan, Peter and I had, for some reason, been taken to a different hospital, Riobamba's biggest. Although the authorities meant well, this turned out to be a fairly painful interlude. Jan had gone ahead but Peter and I, a tatter-demalion duo with makeshift slings and dressings and still dishevelled from our hasty evacuation, were escorted to a second minibus. It would have been kinder to ask us to walk because quite the most agonizing moments of our rescue came when the vehicle left the camp and hit the deep pot-holes of Riobamba's sidestreets. Each jarring bounce threw us out of our seats to hit the roof, and as we tried to hold on to something with one arm the bones in the other crepitated alarmingly. We cried out, but the driver, un-heeding, motored on.

The hospital had been forewarned, but it would have been better if we had surprised them for the casualty ward was soon filled to capacity by the entire staff. Nurses, orderlies, ancillaries, cleaners – all poured in to gawp at *los tres ingleses* and even the doctor on duty, an imperious little fellow, could barely force his way through to shoo them out. Orders were shouted, then countermanded, and we were moved from room to room amid scenes of mounting confusion. Eventually we were taken to three adjoining beds in an upstairs ward. Our clothes and valuables were listed, signed for and removed from us. Thinking that we might be here for some time I began to settle in and even arranged for a young nurse to buy me some postcards of local views and some postage stamps. Jan, meanwhile, was giving them a hard time. A team of nurses tried to fit a catheter and an intravenous drip, but just when they had the needle fairly in he would lash out with his arms, one of which we had now discovered was broken, and send the whole apparatus flying. One time the drip-stand came through the air like a felled factory chimney and I raised my left arm to catch the bottle neatly. Soon Jan's bed was stained with blood and the staff were beginning to realize they had bitten off more than they could chew.

At this point Peter Wills caught up with us. It was reassuring to see his imposing figure stride into the ward in the full tropical dress of a defence attaché, with all the regalia – RAF wings, medal ribbons and aiguillettes – and we sensed immediately that things would be taken in hand.

'I've got a plane to take you all to Quito, so I'll just go and thank the people here and arrange for you to be taken to the airport.'

It proved to be rather difficult to put the hospital machinery into reverse so soon, but presently our possessions were produced and we were propelled in stretcher and wheel-chairs to a side door. Swathed in blankets we were put into cars and though some of the younger girls seemed to be disappointed to lose three such exotic catches I saw a distinct look of relief on Matron's face.

Jeff Aucott had told Colonel Perez to postpone attempts to recover Ron Mace's body, though there were tentative plans to try again in two days' time when the snow might have melted a little. But the pressing need was to get Jan the best possible medical treatment in the quickest possible time and Peter Wills had now prevailed on Colonel Perez to divert an Ecuadorean army Arava from the Viscount search to take him, with the rest of us, to Quito. By 10.30 a.m. we were airborne: Jan on a stretcher with two medical orderlies constantly checking on his condition, Peter Wills, Nick, Peter Chadwick and I on the bench opposite.

'Like a beer?' asked Peter Wills.

Ever resourceful, he had remembered to fill an ice-box with bottles of lager. This was an unexpectedly civilized way to come back to Quito.

12
Scalpel Time

I am sure you will know we are all praying very hard for you.... Judith, Emma, Victoria, Pam, Ruth – and everyone send their love and sincere good wishes. You certainly made the headlines – almost every TV and radio broadcast and newspaper has featured the drama for forty-eight hours now.

letter from John Blashford-Snell, Dover, 17 August 1976

'It never rains but it pours,' as my old nursemaid, Kate Parkinson, used to tell me with a cheerful laugh. After what had happened to the British Vulcan Expedition reconnaissance its members were not really ready for further tragedy on its periphery. But it seemed as if two deaths had not been enough for whatever vindictive Inca gods we had disturbed by attempting to climb Sangay.

One of our principal supports before our arrival in Ecuador, and especially after, had been Dr Brian Kennerley, the gentle, patient head of the British Geological Mission. He and his wife Margaret had housed us and entertained us. Brian had secured us the assistance of the Ecuadorean Department of Geology and Mines in the form of a financial grant and the services of Gerardo Herrera, and arranged for our use of an ODM Land-Rover. It is doubtful whether our scientific projects could have gone ahead without his enthusiastic backing. A day or two after our departure south he set off with Margaret and their two children for a well-earned holiday touring round Colombia, and was almost immediately involved in a car crash somewhere near Cali and killed outright.

My over-riding thought as we digested this dire news was the senselessness of it all:

> As flies to wanton boys, are we to the gods.
> They kill us for their sport.

The very man who, above many others, had done so much to set us on our way, now gone.

It was, of course, very much on the cards that another death might follow. Jan was hanging on to life tenaciously but some fearsome surgery lay ahead if he was to recover fully. None of us could feel sure that he would survive it.

'Iwandziuk in Riobamba, living but in critical condition with head fracture', ran Peter Wills's signal at mid-day Tuesday. Later that night he informed the usual addressees,

I returned to Quito today with the four surviving members of expedition in Army Arava. Lt Iwandziuk, who has been unconscious for most of time since accident and is in serious condition, is in hospital Andrade Marín. Richard Snailham and Peter Chadwick both have fractured right arms but are otherwise fit and in excellent spirits. They are in the Vozandes hospital. Major Cooke has minor injuries to head and leg but was discharged after treatment and is staying with me.

This precise and reasonably hopeful information considerably cheered the friends and relatives of the survivors. For some days they had been wondering what they could do to help and Sarah Iwandziuk had been making plans to fly out posthaste to Ecuador. The Ministry of Defence, in the redoubtable person of Miss Zemla, a veteran civil servant in the Casualty department at Lansdowne House, made enquiries about this. Was it necessary? Would it be helpful? Could it be arranged in time? Peter Wills's reply came back:

Surgeon advises that Iwandziuk has fractured skull and is suffering from dehydration. He is able to answer simple questions only, and probably does not see. His condition is very grave and he could die at any time. He recommends that wife should come if she wishes.

She was already in New York. Her former employer,

Chet Boles, had advanced her the money for a ticket and the Ministry had rushed through her visa and travel documents. Everyone did their bit. The Eastern Airlines pilot even brought his plane down at Miami in a raging storm (which he had planned to avoid by diverting to Orlando) so that she could catch a connecting flight to Quito, and she arrived there early on Thursday 19 August.

As she walked into the arrival hall Nick Cooke and Terry Newenham, the British ambassador's PA, were waiting.

'Thank God Nick's smiling,' she thought. 'That means that Jan's still alive.'

They wasted no time in heading for the vast Andrade Marín hospital and Sarah climbed the flights of stairs to the intensive care unit. The long journey was over and she had made it. But her joy at finding Jan alive was marred by the frightful state in which she found her vital, physically powerful young husband. A horrific image will be fixed in her mind for ever: 'He was lying there curled up in a ball, his head shaved, his skin dehydrated and black and blue with contusions; his head was stitched and covered with dried blood; he looked 150 years old.'

Sarah reeled back in shock, and it was several moments before she could once more view life with some equanimity. She had tried to square up to the facts: Jan was expected to die; his head was like a boiled egg after the first blow from the back of the spoon; he could see nothing and knew nobody – even Sarah was a stranger to him. An operation was scheduled for the next day in which the surgeons were proposing to try to lift the section of skull which was staved in and was pressing on the cerebral cortex.

Jan's appearance was so ghoulish that Sarah sensitively refused to let anyone photograph him. Nick and Peter Wills did what they could to comfort her and it was a great blessing that Terry Newenham, a sympathetic contemporary, asked Sarah to share her flat with her rather than leave her to be lodged in an impersonal hotel. Many times, by day and night, she drove Sarah to and from the Andrade Marín.

The ambassador's tireless PA played a vital role in another respect. Before the fateful day Sarah became aware of a new crisis: Jan was likely to need a great deal of blood to survive the surgery and Quito's hospitals keep limited supplies. Furthermore, Jan's group was A positive – very rare in Ecuador. Sarah herself, though a frequent donor, was of a different group. In despair she spent several hours of the preceding evening telephoning foreign embassies to see if any of their staffs were A positive and prepared to help. There was no response. But happily Terry Newenham, although exhausted after a week of preparing and encipher-ing messages late into the night, and transmitting and receiving them on the Telex machine, was of the same group and gave generously. Other members of the British community also turned out to be, and became donors. The crisis was averted and the operation could go ahead.

It was fortunate for Jan that he had been placed in the hands of a talented and experienced brain surgeon. Dr Herbert Reyes, a neurologist with seven years' training in Baltimore, gave Sarah an immediate feeling of confidence when first she met him. He did not of course admit to her then his privately held view – that Jan would not survive the operation. But survive it he did. He emerged, still in a coma but less delirious, and Dr Reyes suggested that Sarah should sit with him and talk to him in the hope that her voice would ultimately draw forth some response. Des-perately tired, she chatted away at his bedside about their new house at Whitfield, of the old days before their marriage when she lived at East Molesey, about Jasper, their hand-some yellow labrador pup and his voracious appetite for their new furniture.

A day or two later he began to rally and feebly to attempt a few words. But he took Sarah for a nurse and sometimes could recall nothing except his name. His eyes remained firmly shut and he lay in the foetal position uninterested in food or drink.

Then came the magic moment when he understood who Sarah was; magical, even if he could only remember her as

his girlfriend and could not grasp that they were now
married. It pained Sarah to be thus 'divorced' after just six
months and persistently she worked away on his memory.
Gradually it extended backwards and forwards, but he
seemed to have lost all notion of how he came to be on the
mountain or what had happened there. Wisely, Sarah told
him nothing about Adrian and Ron and even though he
was visited only by Nick, Dr Peter Francis and, later on,
by Peter Chadwick and me, he mercifully never asked about
the other two.

'You must have something to eat, darling,' Sarah told
him one day for the umpteenth time. And Jan surprised
her by slowly saying in his flat, Black Country accent, 'Yes.
All right. Some smoked salmon sandwiches, please.' Urged
to drink something he asked for lager and lime. These were
difficult orders to meet in Ecuador and he had to be content
with tuna fish and German beer.

Day by day he improved, but it was still a trying time for
everyone. Sarah and the intensive care unit nurses had to
minister to his every need, and as he lay there with his eyes
still tightly screwed up it became obvious to the doctors
that he was blind. When, very rarely, he opened them there
was no reaction and he quickly closed them again.

But he was now eating well and slowly some strength
returned. His condition, listed first as 'Grave' on the bulletin
board outside the unit, moved to 'Delicate' and then
'Serious'. Sarah remembered feeling how odd it was to be
so pleased at finding him just 'Serious'.

I went once to visit him in the Andrade Marín – a Belsen-
thin figure with a fuzz of blond hair just sprouting again
on his scarred head; his broken right forearm loosely
splinted, a dressing on a lost nail and three of his long,
curled toes black with frostbite.

'Hello, Jan.'

'Hello, Richard.'

We seemed to be back where we were on the mountain,
but although the light, straggly beginnings of a beard
looked strange it was good to see him smile.

There was not much that I felt we could talk about, but Jan warmed to the subject of pretty, brown-eyed Ecuadorean nurses even though he could not see them. Perhaps it was as well because I fear I oversold them. Soon he was being lifted for a few moments into a wheel-chair to exercise some different muscles and to ease his bed sores.

After some days he was moved from the hospital to the Pichincha clinic, a private establishment in the middle of modern Quito. Here, although it proved that we had to pay more to the medical staff, the quality of care was lower and Sarah had to spend fourteen hours a day making sure that he was properly looked after. To lighten her burden we employed a final-year medical student to attend on him at night.

The financial aspects of the expedition were beginning at this time to cause some worry. Although we all believed that we were personally insured Jan, Peter Chadwick and I were nevertheless building up big bills for medical expenses, and it looked as though special arrangements would have to be made to fly Jan home as he could in no way be expected to travel back in the somewhat cramped style offered by Aerovias Quisqueyana.

It was specially cheering to have the help of Peter Francis, who had arrived from Britain shortly after the accident. He, Nick Cooke and Peter Wills worked indefatigably to resolve the problems of hospital bills, flights home and other incidental costs.

Peter Wills at an early stage requested the Ministry of Defence to evacuate the wounded, possibly by routing via Quito one of the regular RAF flights to Belize. Although Miss Zemla and others at the London end did what they could, higher governmental authorities, noting that we were not an officially backed adventure training expedition but merely civilians and military personnel on leave, at first took a correct line and in Pontius Pilate fashion washed their hands of us.

Failing the RAF, Jan would need to recruit his strength in his expensive clinic for a little while longer before being able to take first-class seats (probably four, including Sarah and some medical attendance) by a reputable airline. The rest of us wanted flights much sooner than Jan, the quicker to receive more refined medical treatment at home and to rejoin our families. We had four perfectly good return air tickets (and two promised berths on a Pacific Steam Navigation Company cargo vessel), but they were for specific flights and sailings in mid-September. And the flights were by airlines that were not members of IATA and so the tickets could not easily be exchanged for earlier flights by other airlines, if at all. Such were the complexities with which the defence attaché and the two fitter members of our team were grappling in these last days.

An extra difficulty proved to be the avid interest of the press in what had happened to us. From the moment Peter Chadwick and I touched down at Riobamba we all of us had to deal with the close questioning of reporters in person or by telephone. The ensuing press coverage had three phases: first there were the graphic accounts of our deaths and injuries on the mountain, followed by the dramatic story of the rescue and the removal of the survivors to hospital; then came a period of agonizing reappraisal in which the expedition was alleged to have been mishandled, and its situation in its final days in Quito was grossly misrepresented; lastly came the glow of relief at the return of the survivors to Britain and a series of blow by blow personal accounts in which local boy more or less makes good. Although the third of these phases was generally well conducted, the first two well illustrate how inaccurate some reporting is and how meretricious.

To start with there was the difficulty for men in Fleet Street, and equally in New York, of discovering what had actually happened on a remote outlier of the eastern Andes. Allowably perhaps, the story was garbled – the survivors and the dead being often muddled up, the terrain wrongly described and the volcano's activity sometimes exaggerated. This often derived not so much from the reporters as from their informants, who said what they believed to be true but who could not know our situation exactly. From our embassy in Quito came the notion that at the Royal Military Academy, Sandhurst, I was the Professor of Geology. Ministry of Defence spokesmen and John Blashford-Snell at his Junior Leaders Regiment in Dover made intelligent guesses based on what skimpy information they had. And so the public read of rescuers 'hacking their way through dense jungle' and 'a "forest" of twelve-foot-high tubers' 'like oversized rhubarb' to find the survivors 'hiding in a cave' whilst 'white-hot rocks and lava' rained down on them.

The most consistently accurate reports came from the *Daily Telegraph*, but this was possibly because they were written by Hugh Davies, an old friend from Zaire River Expedition days, and I had sent him, exclusively, a press release on the reconnaissance the day before we had left London.

John Blashford-Snell, though very little acquainted with the plans of the enterprise, took over in his inimitable way and set up a very efficient information centre at Dover. Jan had left an expedition file at his home and this was all John had to go on. It contained descriptions of the first route to Sangay taken by Bonington and Snow – but this had run from the south-east, from Macas, hence the intrusion of the dense jungle and the twelve-foot-high tubers. John kept next of kin and press informed but had very little of substance to be sure of until the rescue was effected. Nevertheless, the office at Dover, constantly manned, was a key point in the lines of communication.

On Thursday, 19 August, our story occupied the front pages of both *Daily Mail* and *Daily Express* under banner headlines. Nick Cooke, staying with Peter and Dorothy Wills, had been telephoned at length by their New York correspondents and was able to give the first full personal story, much of which was printed verbatim. This was the culmination of the first phase of our press coverage, in which the British Vulcan Expedition reconnaissance, a four-days' wonder, had provided newspapermen with some useful copy at a time when they needed it. (In the normal way news runs a bit thin in the dog days.) And Nick Cooke (variously rendered as Major or Mr Nick, Mick or Paul Cooke, Cook, Coake or Cooper, 27, 35 or 37) had become something of a national hero.

But it was all to turn rather sour. On 20 August the *Guardian* introduced the first note of controversy with a report headed 'Climbers "needed volcano expert"' and quoted the views of Dr Basil Booth, a consultant volcanologist, who added that our six-man party should have been split in two with only one group on the mountain at the time, and that group kept well spaced out. But the piece concluded with the opinion of volcanologist Dr Tom Huntingdon: 'The presence of an expert would not necessarily have prevented last week's tragedy.' Of course, we had planned to have Dr Peter Francis with us, but he had been held up for a fortnight by his commitments at the Open University. Furthermore, he felt that of the three volcanoes to be put under review Sangay offered fewest scientific rewards, and Haroun Tazieff was in any case already then known to be going out to study it with a larger, more elaborately equipped team, so Peter Francis was content to concentrate on Sumaco and Reventador. 'I doubt if any volcanologist could have predicted the eruption,' he said later. 'It is sadly ironic that Haroun Tazieff and his party, who had been so self-sacrificing in helping the Sangay rescue, were themselves [just afterwards] caught out by an unexpected eruption on Guadeloupe, though fortunately none of them was severely injured.* From what I had learned of Sangay in Ecuador, and from what I had read from previous accounts of ascents by mountaineers, I was confident that the volcano presented no undue hazards.'

---

* There are no volcanologists with more practical experience at work in the field today than Haroun Tazieff. Although in 1965 he wrote in *The UNESCO Courier*, No. 18, Nov. 1965: 'Few eruptions fail to give some warning signs,' he later came forward with the hypothesis that although some types of eruption, like those on Hawaii, are easily forecast others are not, especially those from volcanoes in the circum-Pacific 'ring of fire', such as Sangay (*The UNESCO Courier*, No. 20, Sept. 1967).

The *Guardian* article also raised the question of 'whether the climbers were wearing hard helmets'. This point was taken up by Tim Ross in a hard-hitting piece in the *Observer* two days later. 'Volcano victims had no helmets' ran the headline uncompromisingly. It was perfectly true; although very well equipped in other respects, we had no climbing helmets. Both Nick Cooke and I had at different times questioned the wisdom of this, but Jan had stuck to his decision not to take them. His grounds for this were two-fold: the first – and weaker – reason was that seven or eight helmets are bulky and would have added considerably to our load both in weight and volume. Secondly, there were no clear precedents for using helmets on a mountain like Sangay. A cone of ash which slopes at 30 to 35 degrees would normally present no problem. Allan Miller writes of the International Andean Mountaineers' ascent of 1975, 'We wore crampons but not helmets, we were not roped.' Of all previous expeditions to scale Sangay the only one for which I have evidence that helmets were worn is the Bonington–Snow ascent of 1968. Few of the risks of injury to the head normally associated with rock climbing and mountaineering would be experienced on Sangay – unless it erupted.* And it is arguable that to be caught underneath a full volcanic eruption means death anyway. In our contingency planning we made no preparations for being so caught, and it is doubtful whether any expedition adequately could.

If not too much time is available, safety on Sangay largely depends on being reasonably lucky, and not in attempting to carry protective gear for the worst possible case. Pick the wrong moment and you are likely to be doomed. It is Russian roulette. As far as can be ascertained we were the first expedition of the nine or ten recorded assaults to pull the trigger on a loaded chamber. As Peter Francis said,

In view of the fact that the volcano was inactive for two or three days before the eruption and two or three days after it, it was

* Some accounts report that when the sun melts the upper snows rocks and stones are 'freed' and bounce down the slopes.

clearly a tragically unfortunate coincidence of timing that led to the party being near the summit when the eruption took place.

All this does not rule out the possibility, however, that in our case had we worn climbing helmets two lives might have been saved and one serious injury averted. It is perfectly arguable that had we done so a vital extra precaution would have been provided at no really great additional inconvenience. Since 12 August 1976, all the survivors and a number of others have pondered on this.

But for the great majority of those whose lives are saved in car smashes by wearing seat belts there are a handful who die by them.

'Tell me,' said Dr Reyes to Sarah one morning, 'was your husband wearing a crash helmet at the time of the accident?'

'Why do you ask?' Sarah replied guardedly.

'No, I am only curious for medical reasons.'

'Well, he wasn't.'

'That's interesting,' said the surgeon thoughtfully, 'because I think that if he had been he would have died of a broken neck.'

Peter Chadwick, in the Vozandes hospital, was taxed by Tim Ross for going to film a volcano which he had himself described as 'extremely active'. We frequently argued the pros and cons of this issue.

'The North End Road is extremely active,' said Peter, 'but I go across it for my fags.'

'Of course you do, because you can see what's coming!'

'Maybe there'll come a time when city pedestrians will have to wear protective armour on a Friday night after eleven, to withstand the drunken drivers. You never know when *they*'re coming at you!'

'No. There's no real analogy. It's more like mountaineers going over a snow bridge across a crevasse, or up a glacier – that's a calculated risk.'

We seemed to agree that, whether or not we had had a volcanologist with us, there would have been some virtue in lingering longer at the foot of Sangay to observe its behaviour.

'In my view,' said Peter Francis afterwards, 'the party made only one mistake – a very understandable one – and that was in not spending more time at the base of the volcano before attempting an ascent. In my briefing, I had advised Iwandziuk of the necessity of establishing the pattern of eruptive activity, but since the party observed *none* of any consequence beforehand, they may have been lulled into a false sense of security.'

Tim Ross also suggested that we had taken the wrong route up Sangay and quoted Minard Hall: 'Nobody knew the route and they took the most dangerous way right into the path of the debris.' This idea was perpetuated by Independent Television on the evening that four of us came back to London Airport: 'Stay with us, and after the break we meet members of the expedition who took the wrong route up a volcano,' the newsman slickly said. We know of only one previous ascent – Bonington and Snow's first – which was not made within the western sector. An approach from Alao or Guarguallá has normally led to climbers tackling the western flank. At present there is a prominent spill of lava on the volcano's north-western face but the west and south-west offer clear snow-fields, and it was up one of these that we climbed. Our route, as it happened, led us towards the rim of the explosive north-western crater which is currently the most active of the three. But exact knowledge of the volcano's present summit formation has only recently become available – from the photographs taken by Minard Hall on the day of our rescue. As Peter Francis has concluded: 'There were certainly other routes, and it is a truism that if the party had been elsewhere at the time of the eruption they would have escaped. *All* routes, however, lead to the summit area and any party near the active crater would stand little chance in the event of an eruption.'

By far the worst example of sensational reporting appeared in the *Daily Mail* from the pen of their New York correspondent. On 28 August he contrived a story to follow up the scoop of nine days earlier. Fixing on a remark of Nick's that we were still in Ecuador waiting with dwindling resources until our flights home could be rearranged, he carried out a relentless probe into our financial and physical health which lasted for several telephone calls. *Mail* sub-editors headed the result 'Volcano Britons "are stranded penniless"' ('Volcano survivors are stranded and broke' in the north of England editions). Nick may have hoped that the newspaper, in return for the story, might come up with some money. If so, we were to be sadly disappointed.

The whole piece was shot through with inaccuracies and false emphases. 'We are having some difficulty exchanging our air tickets for an earlier flight' became 'We just can't get out because we haven't got the money'. The fact that four of us were staying in homes of members of the British community was termed 'living off charity in Ecuador'. And 'my arm has some infection in it' was rendered 'it got infected during my stay in hospital' – an unnecessary and quite false slur on the work of the Vozandes hospital. I was also said to be in danger of losing an arm that had been fractured in six places.

As we later read of Nick Cooke 'going through another kind of hell' it was pleasant to recall those afternoons he and I spent lying in Peter Wills's sun-drenched garden watching the humming-birds flit among the hedges, devouring a paperback, or just staring up at the massive bulk of Pichincha. By and by we would stroll inside, where a log fire had already been lit against the evening's chill and the two Indian maids had already wheeled in the tea. Dorothy Wills would carefully set a cup and saucer at my left hand and we would discuss the day's negotiations at airline offices or Jan's progress in his clinic. Later on, Peter Wills would come home, all bustle, from the embassy and generally invite us to move into a high-vaulted space where he kept the drinks cupboard – 'Sorry about the tonic, but we can't get the genuine stuff here.' I suppose that was the real hell.

13
Exeunt Almost All

The home stretch, the stretch that we know is bound to end, some time, in the rattle of the door-latch, the sudden firelight and the sight of familiar things greeting us as long-absent travellers from far oversea.

Kenneth Grahame, *Wind in the Willows*

Life in those last days in Quito was idyllic enough, and I think we all felt that our financial and travel problems would, as always, resolve themselves in some way. Peter Wills reassured us, for example, that whatever medical bills we ran up would be paid by the embassy as long as we undertook to reimburse H M G later. This was comforting.

We had adequate funds for out-of-pocket expenses and were able to entertain our hosts and buy a few appropriate presents before we left. There was even time for some gentle tourism. Jeff Aucott drove us north to the equator, *La Mitad del Mundo*, whose position had been first fixed by Charles Marie de la Condamine's French expedition of 1735. We saw the great stone monument there, which has unfortunately been built a few hundred yards from the true line, so that all hemisphere-straddlers so far have been deceiving themselves. Whilst there we visited a nearby extinct volcano (a step along the road to recovering our nerve?) and a prehistoric fortified hill-top.

Back in Quito a walk round the old colonial quarter and the heavily gilded La Compañía de Jesús church was a part of my convalescence. But there are eighty-six churches in

the city* and I only had energy for two. We had time to sit
in the sun in the attractive Plaza Independencia watching
colourful *Quiteños* (and *Quiteñas*) pass up and down in front
of the Palacio del Gobierno. Here, at the seat of government, two soldiers, as gaudy as roosters in their early
nineteenth-century gear, stand guard on a colonnaded walk
overlooking the square. Marble plaques on the walls
invariably begin '*Aquí está asesinado el Presidente. . . .*' Heads
of State have now probably been warned off by their
insurers not to stand and make speeches from this vulnerable
vantage point.

We moved round the city tying up loose ends – changing
money at Rodrigo Paz, recording a programme for Ecuadorean Television, having daily injections and changes of
dressings. After the pains and privations of the volcano, it
was a tranquil, relaxed time for most of us. Quito began to
cast a spell, and I came to agree with Christopher Isherwood
that, 'This is a charming city. I wouldn't mind spending six
months here, or even a year.'

The home stretch is often as satisfying a part of an expedition as any other. Whilst the days are tinged with sadness at
the prospect of leaving an interesting corner of the world
to return to humdrum, workaday reality, that very reality
begins to exert a gnawing appeal. Familiar things swim
back into the consciousness, the stuff of ordinary life seems
attractive, tiny worries form. I called to mind a talk on the
expedition that I had undertaken to give in Chertsey on
14 September. Would I be out of hospital in time?

One of the fascinations of expeditions is in the contrasts
to normal life that they afford, and ours had offered as stark
a set as any I could recall: how much more delightful a bed
with sheets on it after nights spent in pools of water on the
hard lava of Sangay's shoulder. How much more appetizing
a fried English breakfast after three weeks of lumpy
porridge or a mug of watery coffee or, latterly, nothing at
all.

* *The South American Handbook*, 1977. But Christopher Isherwood says
fifty-seven, including monasteries. Can they have built thirty since 1949?

We were already becoming happily adjusted to civilization again and parts of it were very British. One familiar
evening occurred at El Pub Inglés, next door to the embassy.
Nick, Peter Chadwick, Peter Francis and I stood in the
crowded bar with Jeff Aucott, Dennis Thornley, the British
chargé d'affaires, and we entertained Haroun Tazieff,
Isabelle Garma and the other French and Ecuadorean
scientists, now back from the mountain on which they had
so sustained us.

Baulked at Sangay, Tazieff was now off to look at the
volcano Soufrière on the French island of Guadeloupe,
which was showing signs of renewed activity.

It was a time for much more rational, considered, less
emotional discussion of what had happened to us on the
mountain. An enthralled circle of lay listeners surrounded
Tazieff and Francis, dazzled by the flow of volcanological
erudition. I suppose I understood about seven words in ten.
If I had known, however, that I had just been appointed
to a Chair of Geology at Sandhurst I would have tried
harder. Soon, however, the lava palaver began to range
world-wide and Tazieff, a seasoned, outdoor type who
seemed not quite to belong in a smoke-filled pub with
walls and a roof, told of some of his earlier exploits.

A Belgian, he was a geologist by training and had first
got close to his subject matter by climbing high in the Alps
and pot-holing deep into the Pyrenees. His first great
adventure was the descent of the deepest cave in the world,
the Gouffre de la Pierre Saint-Martin, to 2389 feet, in a
series of explorations between 1951 and 1953. Volcanoes
next caught his interest – and have retained it. He has
explored and filmed Etna, Stromboli and Virounga whilst
they were in eruption, and studied an astonishing number
of others around the globe. In Kivu once, he spent the night
alone inside the crater of Nyiragongo, the only volcano in
the world with a permanently fluid lava lake.

His experiences included tragedy and he knew well
enough how we felt about Adrian and Ron. In 1952, whilst
deep underground in the Gouffre de la Pierre Saint-Martin

on the Franco-Spanish border, a cable hoisting his friend
Marcel Loubens up the shaft had snapped. Loubens had
plummeted several yards onto a heap of boulders and many
hours later he had died, his spine shattered. Tazieff was
below with him all the time, but he carried on the exploration of the Gouffre Lépineux and was the last to leave the
cave system.

These pioneering descents were being made while fellow
undergraduate Brian Simpson and I were tentatively
groping our way down Long Kin East in the Yorkshire
moors. Not long after, we had sat and gasped at Tazieff's
Volcano, in which, like Matthew Arnold's Empedocles, he
had plunged into the crater of Etna – but with a cine-
camera. Talking to Tazieff was, for me, a trip into
history.

Our farewells were genuinely warm. We exchanged
addresses. Yes, we would keep in touch. But the news from
Guadeloupe was ominous. Active since July, Soufrière now
bore all the signs, experts said, of building up to a mammoth
eruption – of a force equalling several atomic bombs. Over
72000 people had already evacuated Basse-Terre, the island's
capital, at the volcano's foot. 'The eruption is now an
inexorable process,' Professor Brousse said – and it had
been expected for ten days or more. So Haroun Tazieff and
his team must hurry north to Guadeloupe. The best of
British luck, we said.

We had very little more to do. Air France had given us
tickets for 1 September. On our final morning we visited
Jan at the Pichincha clinic. Nick had promised that he
would shave him, and Jan, in soldierly fashion, chafed to
be rid of his few whiskers. It was a cheerful scene as Nick
deftly applied the lather, and it contrasted sharply with the
last time I had watched a patient shaved. This had been in a
Bournemouth hospital when a barber on his rounds was
tidying up a very old man, a Mr Wilkinson, formerly a
respected local solicitor. In that callous way that hospital
patients often have with each other a joky amputee had
come up to the cot on his crutches and shouted, 'Havin'

your last shave then, Wilky? Eh?' But for Jan now it was his first, and a token of his steady improvement.

The Air France jet bore us off to Bogotá. Shortly afterwards we were in the heat and humidity of Caracas. As we lifted up again over the turquoise Caribbean a click was heard on the intercom.

'This is your captain here. I regret to have to inform passengers that we have developed a slight malfunction in the navigational computer . . .'

Nick, the two Peters and I exchanged nervous glances.

'. . . and we will be coming down to make repairs – in Guadeloupe.'

Envoi

And all shall be well and
All manner of thing shall be well
When the tongues of flame are in-folded
Into the crowned knot of fire
And the fire and the rose are one.

T. S. Eliot, 'Little Gidding', Four Quartets

Possibly the loneliest person in Ecuador during the first week of September was Sarah Iwandziuk. Her happy homecoming had to be postponed until Jan became air-portable and their tickets had been fixed.

Miss Zemla, Peter Wills and many others played a sterling role here and eventually Jan and Sarah were booked to take a scheduled flight to Miami. She had a problem getting him into the aircraft as he could not manage the steps. Otherwise the journey went well. In Florida the United States Air Force took over and they were driven to a hospital on the base at Homestead, where Jan responded favourably to the English-speaking nurses.

Twenty-four hours later Sarah thrilled to the sight of the Royal Air Force roundels on a VC 10, which arrived complete with emergency operating theatre and surgeon. Happily, neither was needed and, suffused with relief, she watched Jan laugh and make simple jokes as they winged across the Atlantic, over Land's End and past the illuminated Severn Bridge. It was an emotional return.

Nick, the two Peters and I had earlier arrived in London to emotion of a different sort – an acrimonious meeting of airport officials, Ministry of Defence Public Relations people and mediamen, followed by a wearisome, tendentious television interview.

Peter Francis and Nick had gone sadly home, Peter Chadwick into Charing Cross Hospital – and just as quickly out again, discharged as having an arm well on the way to normal recovery, and I had been conveyed to the Royal Herbert Military Hospital in Woolwich, the top army bone place. I spent nine days there while the infection in my arm was further reduced and X-ray pictures taken. Towards the end Jan joined me in the same hospital.

After a day or two an operation implanted a plate in his right forearm and amputated part of two frostbitten toes.

'What colour's this dressing gown I'm wearing, Jan?' I asked when I called into his room some time after. It was a brilliant royal blue.

'Not sure, old son,' he said. 'Have a beer. Got plenty here, somewhere . . .'

His eyes were open now, but he could see only blurs, and colours eluded him completely. But there was some vision there and it seemed to be getting better all the time.

Soon he was discharged and his return visits to the hospital became fewer. As 1977 progressed he turned to the task of sorting out the many thorny problems which the reconnaissance left in its wake. Because of Jan's earlier incapacity Lieutenant-Colonel David Hall had produced a report to which many of us contributed. Peter Francis and Peter Wills wrote others for the Royal Society and the Ministry of Defence. Jan had still to grapple with questions of insurance, medical expenses, lost equipment, as well as his own slow physical recovery.

There came a time when the overall record of the expedition had to be looked at. How did we stand? On the debit side, two men dead, three others badly injured, much of our gear left behind; to our credit, one third of a reconnaissance somewhat patchily completed – a shaky foundation for any further endeavour, but something. The Royal Society had given Peter Francis a large grant, and the Royal

Geographical Society and the Mount Everest Foundation had given the expedition itself others. We wondered whether they would feel they had had value for money. No doubt they are accustomed to the occasional venture which for one reason or another does not deliver the goods.

Soon we had to consider the question of whether there would be, as planned, a follow-up expedition. Putting the reconnaissance in its perspective, after a year things seemed more hopeful than they had at the time it had ended. It looked as if it need not be written off as an unmitigated disaster. There was work still to be done in the Ecuadorean Andes. The geological uncertainties remained. Peter Francis had a continuing interest in our three volcanoes, whose scientific secrets were still to be unravelled. We had started something which perhaps ought to be finished.

But the scientific motive was by no means paramount, not even dominant in most of us. Why might we choose to go again? I have often thought it somewhat spurious to justify continued activity after an expedition fatality on the grounds that the dead man would have wished it so. I suspect this generally means that the living themselves, deep down, wish it so and hope that he also would have wished it so. Nevertheless, would it not be better in our case that the loss of two dear friends should lead on to some sort of satisfactory achievement, rather than to nothing? And there was a natural wish to perpetuate the memory of these men.

If Ingrid Cranfield were ever to write a supplement to *The Challengers* our activities would very likely be considered for her Science/Culture category, 'Looking for Results'.* But how important to us was an end product? Motives are always something of a mystery. Ours had been individual and differing, though perhaps overlapping one with another. 'The achievement is little;' wrote Mrs Cranfield, 'the conception and commitment are all.' The reconnaissance team had been strongly enough committed to the

* *The Challengers: British and Commonwealth Adventure since 1945*, Weidenfeld and Nicolson, 1976.

scientific aims; but the quest-for-adventure, getting-away-from-it-all element had been the most powerful driving force. The Ulysses factor, rather than love for pure science, had prevailed. This factor was unquenched and would probably operate again.

I personally felt drawn by the prospect of returning. On brief acquaintance I had liked Ecuador and the Ecuadoreans, who cannot be blamed for their volcano's wretched sense of timing. One of the disappointments of the reconnaissance had been that its early abandonment had curtailed any study of or involvement with the country and its people. I did not aim to become a 'six-weeks' expert' but if our visit had run its full term I felt I could have written and talked about Ecuador itself with more depth and assurance. I was at risk of seeming like one of those 'If-it's-Tuesday-this-must-be-Belgium' tourists.

It would be an emotional experience in itself to return to Sangay, and I am often asked if I would climb it again. Perversely, the brooding monster exercises a sort of macabre fascination. I should like to see it again, but I should not want to climb it. The haunting memory of Ron Mace, under his blanket of snow and ash, would deter me. While the scientists went about their business with hammers and gas jars I should wait below in the base camp and have some tea ready for them when they came back.

The attitudes of other survivors may vary. One who would have every justification for never climbing Sangay again would be Nick Cooke. On 7 March 1977, the second supplement to the *London Gazette* announced the Queen's approval of the award to Nick of the George Medal. The citation told the story of his grim experience on the mountain and concluded that he had 'acted with the greatest selflessness and courage to keep the injured going throughout the five days which followed the eruption'. He spent 1977 training his beloved Gurkhas in the New Territories of Hong Kong and has probably earned a rest from active volcanoes.

With a rare determination, Jan Iwandziuk doggedly turned to the prospect of concluding our unfinished project. But although physically strong again he was not yet properly fit. A blind spot in the lower right-hand sector of his field of vision still prevented him from driving on the public roads. So the army transferred him from the demanding task of commanding a troop at the Junior Leaders Regiment to the quieter pastures, still within the Royal Engineers, of the Postal and Communications Centre at Mill Hill.

Here he began to plan for an expedition which he knew that he would not himself be able to lead. I offered him my support, though my own active participation depended, equally, on a return to complete fitness. Dr Guillermo Guerra, at the Vozandes hospital, had diagnosed a compound, comminuted fracture of the right humerus and had picked out, in a first operation, a great many shivered, splintered fragments of bone that could never be properly reassembled.

'You will be all right,' he had told me. 'They are now putting very good plastic joints in the elbow.'

The head of the radius and the ulna were also found to be shattered and so in May 1977, Colonel Gordon Small at the Royal Herbert Military Hospital, removed various chunks of calcareous growth and fitted a prosthetic elbow of, in fact, stainless steel. In June a third operation put my right arm on the slow road to normal service. It was possible to think of Ecuador 1978.

We could not pretend, however, that things were really normal. 12 August 1976 had been a turning point in the lives of all four survivors. Sangay had left its mark and we were changed men, physically and psychologically. There was less buoyancy and insouciance in the way we prepared for the expedition proper. Memories of Adrian Ashby-Smith and Ron Mace cast long, sombre shadows over all our proceedings and frequently gave us pause. We privately grieved for our dead friends and we were sad for their bereaved families.

But we were not totally discouraged by the outcome of the reconnaissance. We set ourselves challenges in life. Sometimes we meet them, but sometimes they defeat us. It is perhaps better to be defeated by them once in a while than not to set them at all.

Bibliography

Bemelmans, Ludwig, *The Donkey Inside*, Hamish Hamilton, 1947.

Bonington, Chris, *The Next Horizon*, Victor Gollancz, 1973.

Brooks, John (Ed.), *The 1977 South American Handbook*, Trade and Travel Publications, Bath, 1976.

Bullard, Fred M., *Volcanoes of the Earth*, Rev. Edn. Austin and London, University of Texas Press, 1976.

Dyott, G. M., 'The Volcanoes of Ecuador, Guideposts in Crossing South America', *National Geographic Magazine*, vol. LV, no. 1, Jan. 1929.

Flornoy, Bertrand, *Jivaro*, Elek Books, 1953.

Francis, Peter, *Volcanoes*, Penguin Books, 1976.

Gunther, John, *Inside South America*, Hamish Hamilton, 1967.

Hemming, John, *The Conquest of the Incas*, Macmillan, 1970.

Isherwood, Christopher, *The Condor and the Cows*, Methuen, 1949.

Lewis, G. Edward, 'El Sangay, Fire-breathing Giant of the Andes', *National Geographic Magazine*, vol. 97, no. 1, Jan. 1950.

Moore, Robert Thomas, 'The First Ascent of El Sangay', *Natural History*, parts 1 and 2, May and June 1950.

Neumann Van Padang, M. (Ed.), *Catalogue of the Active Volcanoes of the World including Solfatara Fields, Part XIX, Colombia, Ecuador and Peru*, International Association of Volcanology, Rome, 1966.

Snailham, Richard, *The Sangay Tragedy*, Geographical Magazine, vol. L, no. 2, Nov. 1977.

Snow, Sebastian, *Half a Dozen of the Other*, Hodder and Stoughton, 1972. 'Into the Mouth of an Erupting Volcano', *Daily Telegraph Magazine*, 104, Sept. 23 1966.

Tazieff, Haroun, *Caves of Adventure*, Hamish Hamilton, 1953. *Craters of Fire*, Hamish Hamilton, 1952. *Ma Nuit dans el Vulcan du Niragongo*, Marco Polo (Paris), 12, 1955. *The Menace of 'extinct' Volcanoes*, The UNESCO Courier, 20, 1967. *La Soufrière et Autres Volcans*, Flammarion, Paris, 1978.

Whymper, Edward, *Travels among the Great Andes of the Equator*, Charles Knight, 1972.

APPENDIX A
Underneath the Andes

Since the days of Charles Marie de la Condamine in the mid-eighteenth century and Alexander von Humboldt and Charles Darwin in the nineteenth, the Andes have held a fascination for scientists. Geologists, and to a lesser extent zoologists and botanists, have since then abounded, and their interest in the great mountain range is still evident. The fact that Haroun Tazieff, Minard Hall and Peter Francis were all planning to home in on the same mountain at more or less the same time is its own testimony. Why was it that these three volcanologists were drawn to Sangay? To find the answer to this a word or two has to be said about the geological significance of the area and about volcanoes generally.

In the late 1920s the theory was put forward that the earth's mantle, the material underlying the thirty-kilometre-thick crust, was not solid but as viscous as toffee or pitch, and maintained at high temperatures by the decay of radioactive elements. The theory further postulated that convection currents, created by differences of temperature within the mantle, would over millions of years move the rocks of the mantle with imperceptible slowness around a circular course, hot ones moving upwards, cooler ones down.

Running from north to south down the middle of the Atlantic and Pacific oceans are two ridges noted for intense volcanic and seismic activity. Drillings showed that the rocks below the ocean bed were hottest near these central ridges and coolest near the continental land masses on either side of them. In the 1960s it suddenly dawned on geologists that the hot rocks rising from the mantle split apart at these ridges (which were themselves pushed up in places far enough to break the sea's surface at points like Tristan da Cunha and Easter Island) and then moved east and west along the ocean bed like a conveyor belt, carrying the rocks of the ocean floor with them. This 'sea-floor spreading' theory was well enough, but there was a snag. Geologists reckoned a new floor could be laid under all the world's oceans in, say, 200 million years. But the earth is at least twenty times as old as this. Where did all the old rocks go? Answer: as they cooled off they were drawn down into the earth's mantle again, in the deep ocean trenches.

Now all this thrusting up and grinding down could not go on without a great deal of heat being generated – enough to melt some of the rocks that abraded against one another, and turn them into magma. Some of this magma would be forced high enough, under sufficient pressure, to burst through the earth's crust in places, like pustules on an adolescent's neck. Hence more volcanoes.

It was soon realized that the 'sea-floor spreading' theory also supported the old idea of continental drift. Brazil had long since been observed to fit neatly into the Gulf of Guinea. Now there was a theory which could explain how it might once have done so. The whole of the earth's surface was soon divided up, like the portions of a tortoise's carapace, into irregular areas or plates. These were said to touch each other at 'constructive plate margins' – in the places where the hot mantle rocks were forced up to the sea bed to become crust. Where the cooling crust rocks were pushed down under a continental land mass was termed a 'destructive plate margin'.

South America is bounded on its western side by the Nazca, or East Pacific plate. This plate is born way out at sea as it emerges along a line running north from Easter Island. It moves eastward at the rate of a few centimetres a year, slowly cooling, and then plunges down into the Chile–Peru Ocean Trench and finally underneath the Andes at an angle of about 25 degrees.

This western edge of South America is, therefore, often cited as a classic example of an oceanic/continental destructive plate margin. Yet for such a major feature of the earth's crust the detailed geology of the Andes is surprisingly poorly known.

Scattered about the 8000-kilometre length of the Andean cordillera are thousands of extinct or dormant volcanoes and among them are about forty-five which have shown evidence of activity in 'historic' times, within the past 10000 years, that is. There are three distinct belts of active Andean volcanism: northern, central and southern. The central and southern parts have been studied with some thoroughness recently but the northernmost part, in Ecuador and Colombia, still awaits really close examination. The central belt seems quiescent, and there may have been only one large-scale eruption there since Francisco Pizarro arrived with his conquistadors to defeat the Incas in the 1530s.

A great deal more activity is found in the northern and southern belts – in Ecuador/Colombia and in southern Chile. But there is a difference between them. Volcanoes along the Chile–Argentine border like Nevado Ojos del Salado and Osorno are not often spectacularly active, although there have been a few big eruptions in southern Chile during the last two generations. On the other hand, two of the volcanoes in Ecuador are as constantly active as any in the world, and the more rumbustious of them is certainly Sangay, with records of almost continuous eruptions dating back to 1628 (see Appendix C). Reventador is a lively second in the active list.

So there was good reason to study the hyper-sensitive volcanoes of the northern belt, and specially so since the above-mentioned two, with Sumaco – which seems dormant now but is believed to have been active in historic times – are much more remote and thus less visited than the classic giants of the northern belt, Chimborazo, Cotopaxi and the like.

We intended to mount a scientific expedition to try and

learn more about the nature of eruptions at our three selected sites, and particularly to determine if there was any pattern to their activity. We hoped to be able to estimate the volume of erupted material over a period of time and thus find the rate of magma production of our two active specimens in cubic kilometres per year. Andean volcanoes are thought to be in general much less productive than those at constructive plate margins, as in Iceland, for example. One hundred cubic metres of material is spewed out each year in Hawaii – a volcanic complex located right in the middle of a plate, and one that has been closely watched over the last century.

While the rest of the Andes goes in for a few eruptions quite big in volume, Ecuador seems to experience a large number of relatively small ones. This could be because volcanoes like Sangay are chemically different. The rocks it ejects are basaltic andesite (with about fifty-six per cent silicon dioxide) as opposed to the andesite of others further south in the cordillera. This means that the viscosity of the upthrust magma is a good deal less (the toffee is a little more chewy) and thus it can be erupted more easily.*

A collection of rocks from different places and at different depths on the slopes of Sangay might reveal if there have been any changes in their composition over the years. Central Andean rocks have a quite wide range, the earliest *ejecta* often being basaltic andesite and the latest andesite. It is suspected that Sangay would produce a more limited range.

Furthermore, the chemistry of its rocks would be interesting *per se*. Andesite erupted in the central belt seems to have originated in the partial melting of the mantle below the continental crust but to have been somewhat contaminated by the molten rocks of that crust. However, the strontium

* The difference between constipation and diarrhoea is too extreme to provide a good analogy here – apart from its indelicacy – but volcanic *ejecta* do vary in the same sort of way and it is tempting to suggest that Ecuadorean volcanoes, were they human, could do with a good dose of Lomotil, whilst the central Andean ones need cascara.

isotope data that exists shows that the rocks erupted in Ecuador have not been so contaminated but come purely from the mantle. This, we felt, needed further investigation – the results were based on only a few samples. Perhaps we could in some small way help to resolve the controversy as to whether andesite magma comes from the upper mantle, the descending oceanic plate or the continental crust.

Geochemical analysis of the rocks of our three volcanoes was necessary to correlate them not only with those from other parts of the Andes, but with those from other areas of the Ecuadorean cordillera. There is thought to be considerable variation from west to east across it, in the ratio of silicon to potassium and in other trace element data. Sumaco was specially interesting here because two analyses made in the 1920s by the Americans R. J. Colony and Joseph H. Sinclair suggest that this young volcano, lying far out to the east of the cordillera surrounded by the forests of the Amazonian basin, is quite different in its make-up from any other so far studied in the Andes.

After the expedition proper it should be possible, we believed, to write a volcanic history of Sangay. Are there older craters around the cone? How extensive are the deposits of pyroclastic rocks? These were questions that would have to be answered by any such historian. A detailed map of the volcano could also be drawn. Only a crude representation occurs on the 1 : 50000 map of the area. Air photographs exist of all our three volcanoes, and these would help to counter the difficulties posed by the thick forest cover on Reventador and Sumaco. The maps could well show the range and spread of the different types of volcanic product – lava, pyroclastic rocks, mud, ash and so on.

Volcanologists would be interested, too, in the temperatures of the erupted lava, if any, and the grain size distribution of ash falls around the active volcanoes. But the most demanding task that was suggested to us was to collect gas samples from the fumaroles and vents near or at the summits of Sangay and Reventador. This was something that Haroun Tazieff, with his highly specialized equipment, was trying to do.

I had memories of the little-understood experiments that I once conducted with gas jars in the fume chambers of the labs at Oakham. From time to time a tiny fantasy took root in my mind: would the baleful eye of old Hitchcock, my chemistry master, be on me as I advanced up Sangay's seething lava with my gas jar? Trapping concentrated sulphur dioxide at over three miles above sea level was hardly my line. Having failed Physics-with-Chemistry at 'O' Level I would be bound once again to make a bosh of the Practical, and in any case the technology would be so much more complicated today. At all events, I do not suppose that I shall ever now know at first hand how the gases will some day be collected.

Note left at base camp by Gerardo Herrera at 2 a.m., 13 August

(author's translation)

Camp at the foot of Sangay

At four in the afternoon on Thursday, 12 August, to our great surprise we heard cries of distress from the mountain. And so Anacleto Guambo, Ramón Tenemasa and I then began to look for them, since at one o'clock we had from the base camp seen an enormous eruption. At 5.30 p.m. we met Peter Chadwick in a ravine, his right arm broken and head injured, and he told us that the eruption had over-whelmed them at the top of the volcano, hurling them down its sides. At 6.15 p.m. we rescued Richard Snailham also, his right arm broken. Both Englishmen were taken to the base camp and put under the care of Anacleto Guambo and Ramón Tenemasa who were our guides. At 6.30 p.m. the guides who were with the French expedition arrived and from that time they began to join in the search for the other lost Englishmen and two of them will come with me to Plaza Pamba in search of help.

The tragedy took place at 4850 metres. For the further information of the search and rescue teams the missing men were dressed in red, carrying green rucksacks and climbing ropes, blue and red ice-axes and cameras and cinefilm. Their names are:

	Nick Cooke	50 years
	Aidrian Ashby	35 years
(Leader)	Jan Iwandzink	32 years
	Ron Mace	30 years

Departure had been at 6 a.m. for they planned to reach the crater by twelve and come back early, so as to set off towards Guargualla on the morning of Friday.

For further information apply to Anacleto Guambo for he knows the route they took yesterday and indeed today, which you will perhaps find marked by red flags. Please follow these signs!

The base camp with all that they have there I leave in the care of Anacleto Guambo and Ramón Tenemasa. I will myself give more information at Riobamba or at the Hacienda at Guargualla.

Yours   Gerardo Herrera   Mining Engineer

Ministry of Natural Resources

This message was left very sensibly by Gerardo with Anacleto to hand by way of explanation to any Ecuadoreans who might arrive at our base camp after he had gone.

He was wrong about the proposed time of our departure for Guargualla. We had hoped to carry out further reconnaissances for another full day.

He misspelled a couple of names and he also overestimated our ages by up to forty per cent. It would have been interesting to know how old he reckoned Chadwick and myself. – G.R.S.

APPENDIX C

Edited extract from the *Catalogue of the Active Volcanoes of the World including Solfatara Fields, Part XIX, Colombia, Ecuador and Peru*, by G. Hantke and A. Parodi I. (International Association of Volcanology, Rome, 1966)

i. NAME AND LOCATION

Name of the volcano: Sangay (15, 2–9)
Synonyms: Sanagay
Name of the crater: [none known]
Type of the volcano: Compound Strato Volcano
Location: Provincia Oriental Morrona Santiago, Ecuador
Geographical position: Lat 2° 00′ South
                         Long 78° 20′ West
Height above sea level: 5323 m (Stübel, 1897)
                          5230 m (Atlas histor.-geogr. del
                             Ecuador, 1960)
Height above the northern base: 1700 m
Height above the southern base: 1500 m

ii. FORM AND STRUCTURE

It shows an almost symmetrical form with a very young, smooth and barren surface covered with fragmented material from recent eruptions. The summit is capped with snow and ice. The height of 5323 m was measured by W. Reiss in 1872; it has, however, increased since then. Sangay is composed of an alternation of tephra and lava flows.

At its eastern base the tropical forest begins, and stretches without break eastward to the Atlantic. On the other three sides great ash plains, surrounding the cone, have been produced by the volcano mainly in the last few centuries.

These ash plains have been sculpted by almost constant rains into a labyrinth of black canyons, 150 to 600 m deep.

In August 1929 Moore ascended Sangay in a period of the volcano's dormancy. At that time the cone was perfect, greatly in contrast with the truncated top drawn by Whymper fifty years before. The main axis of the central crater extends from north-west to south-east, the diameter being about 270 m. The highest point of the crater rim is situated to the west; the lower rim, with its broad, deep breach, lies on the north-eastern side. Through this notch the youngest lava flows have streamed into a deep gorge on the eastern flank. Numerous fumaroles occur within and around the crater, which must have repeatedly changed in shape by constant eruptions between 1934 and the present day.

iii. VOLCANIC ACTIVITY

The volcano has probably, with no very great interruptions, been continuously active from 1728 until about 1916 and again from 1934 to the present (1960). The eruptive activity consists of a frequent occurrence of explosive outbursts and occasional lava flows. Usually the explosions take place at intervals of some minutes to several hours. Strombolian activity is often observed, greater outbursts more seldom. The ash clouds are carried by constant winds westward to the Pacific or eastward to Brazil.

The following data indicates only activity which was observed and recorded:

Dates	Activity in central crater	Normal explosion	Lava flow	Remarks
1728				After a long period of quiescence,* activity started in Sept. or Oct. with a violent explosion and ash rains in Rio-bamba
1738	★	★		March. Strong activity
1739	★	★	★	Violent eruptions. Ejection of incandescent bombs; glow was seen frequently, detonations were heard 200 km away. Lava flow in April
1740	★	★		
1742	★	★	★?	Glow was seen frequently
1743	★	★	★	
1744	★	★		Intense activity
1745	★	★		
1797	★	★		
1801	★	★		
1802	★	★		
1842	★	★		Heavy ash rains
1843	★	★		Big ash explosions; detonations heard 300–400 km away
1849	★	★		December. Explosions every 14 seconds. Thunder heard 600 km south-westward
1854	★	★	★?	August. Fireglare on the top

* Sangay is now known to have been active exactly a century earlier (see p. 110).

Dates	Activity in central crater	Normal explosion	Lava flow	Remarks
1856	★	★		February 12. Major eruptions
1858	★	★		December
1859	★	★		May. Strombolian activity, explosions every 10–15 mins
1860	★	★		
1861	★	★		
1867	★	★		
1868	★	★		
1869	★	★	★	Eruptive clouds rose 7000 m above the crater
1870	★	★	★	
1871	★	★	★	
1872	★	★	★	Volcano observed in May, October, November and December. In November a central cone grew inside the summit crater, the rim of which was breached on the south-east
1873	★	★	★	November, December
1874	★	★	★	
1879	★	★		December
1880	★	★		January. Intense activity
1903	★	★		June, August. Important eruptions. Smoke columns reached heights of 10000–11000 m; on 13 July, 13000 m above the crater

Dates	Activity in central crater	Normal explosion	Lava flow	Remarks
1916				About this year eruptive activity ceased and volcano became dormant
1923, 1929				Fumarolic activity observed
1934	★	★		August 8. Strong explosions began new activity
1935	★	★		Heavy ash rains in July
1936	★	★		August
1937	★	★	★	April. Big ash eruptions and probably *nuées ardentes.** May 2–5, lava flow. November, intense activity
1938	★	★		September
1940	★	★		
1943	★	★		Glow was seen. Strombolian activity
1944	★	★		
1946	★	★		September
1948	★	★		
1949	★	★		
1950	★	★		December. Heavy ash rains, glow, rumblings, earthquakes
1960	★	★		January, intense activity

* In a *nuée ardente* a foaming mass of superheated gases and incandescent solid particles spill down the volcano's sides like a saucepan of milk boiling over.

iv. PETROGRAPHY

The rocks of the volcano are andesite and basalt according to Tannhaüser (Reiss *und* Stübel, 1904).

These rocks consist of:

Lava layers of pyroxene andesites at 3700 and 4450 m above sea level.

A lava layer of olivine-bearing pyroxene andesite at 3700 m above sea level and fresh bombs between an altitude of 4200 and 4900 m.

Olivine-bearing augite andesite in the Quebrada Singuna Sanchez.

Olivine basalt from a young lava flow in the Quebrada de la Chorrera at 4197 m above sea level with 51.41% silica.

APPENDIX D
Nick Cooke's Citation

From: Second Supplement to
THE LONDON GAZETTE
of 7 March 1977

MINISTRY OF DEFENCE: HONOURS AND AWARDS

The QUEEN has been graciously pleased to approve the
award of the George Medal to the undermentioned:

Major Paul Nicholas COOKE (445823), 10th Princess Mary's
Own Gurkha Rifles.

Major Cooke was a member of the six-strong British
Vulcan Expedition reconnaissance team which went to
investigate three volcanoes in Ecuador in August–September 1976.

Whilst climbing at 16,000 ft. on the first of these—the
17,500 foot Mount Sangay—the volcano erupted, showering
all six climbers with hot volcanic rocks and knocking them
from their footholds on the snow. Cooke, with the other
five, slid 1,500 feet down the smooth, 35° slopes of the
mountain. It was mid-day on 12th August 1976.

Although struck on the head and leg, Cooke had been
least badly wounded of all and immediately took over
control of the team. Two men were sent 4,000 feet down
the mountain to the base camp to organise help and Cooke
stayed with three survivors who had severe head injuries.

All afternoon Cooke tended the wounded. One died
quite soon; the remaining two he placed in survival bags
and administered to their needs. As night fell he lay on the
snow clutching the survival bags and flashing a torch to

mark his position. The cold was intense and sleep virtually impossible.

Shortly after dawn he tied the survivors together and set off for the base camp—becoming as lost in a maze of near-vertical-sided ravines as had been the two who had gone down the previous day.

He reached camp in an enfeebled state, but immediately began to clean and dress the wounds of the two survivors now there. Some porters meanwhile went to fetch in the two men on the mountain, but one died on the way down. The other he placed in the drier of the two tents and began to clean, warm and feed him. The weather now deteriorated, the porters left, and Cooke, alone, struggled to prepare hot food and keep the wounded alive.

Two days of lashing rain and high winds ensued. Food supplies ran out, the survivors' wounds were becoming infected and Cooke realised he would have to try to reach the camp of a French expedition which he knew to have been placed a mile to the north, across a river.

But the river, once placid, was now swollen and impassable. Cooke nevertheless waded in. He was bowled over by the force of icy water. After a second attempt he thought it more prudent to return. Rescue came later that night.

Major Cooke acted with the greatest selflessness and courage to keep the injured going throughout the five days which followed the eruption.

Index

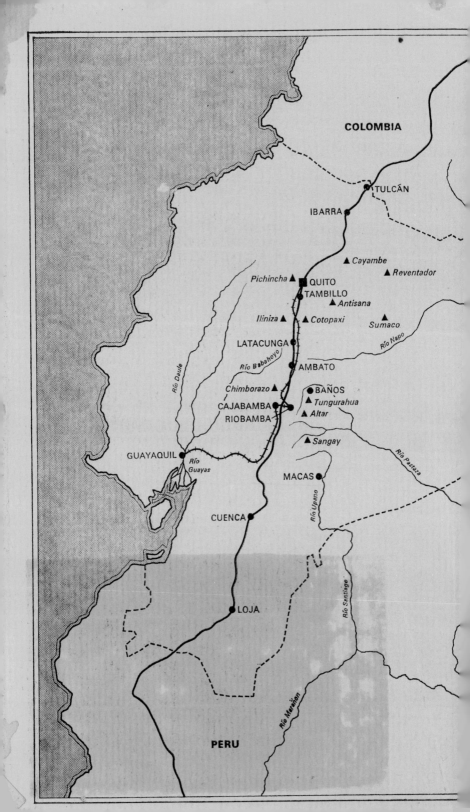